Praise for *Unfear* and Gaurav Bhatnagar and Mark Minukas

The lifeblood of the modern organization is the capacity of its people to create and innovate and keep pushing the boundaries of what is possible. While we acknowledge that doing this is fraught with uncertainty and risk, what we don't acknowledge or talk about in organizations is the fear and the dysfunction it causes. In this timely and much-needed book, Gaurav Bhatnagar and Mark Minukas share their learnings from more than 30 years of working with leaders and organizations to achieve break-through performance. They offer insightful advice on how to unfear—to fundamentally shift our relationship with fear and use it as a tool for learning and growth, both personally as individuals and systemically as leaders of organizations. This book will transform how you live your life and how you lead your teams and organization. A must-read!

 —SEAN AGGARWAL, Chairman of the Board of Directors of Lyft

In *Unfear*, you will read how Gaurav Bhatnagar responds to a personal transformational opportunity with great skepticism, sarcasm, and disdain. We've all been there, haven't we? Could a moment really transform a person? Could reading a book? With Bhatnagar and Minukas as your Sherpas, the answer is yes—and this is that book. Crack it open with skepticism; close it having been transformed. This is the moment you've been waiting for. Take it. You won't regret it. You'll be forever changed.

 —RICHARD SHERIDAN, CEO and Chief Storyteller
of Menlo Innovations and author of *Joy, Inc.:*
How We Built a Workplace People Love

Many of us charged with charting a path toward sustainable growth—a path that taps into the diversity, authenticity, and genius of all our employees—struggle to find the right way to express and build the type of culture this requires. Terms such as *risk taking, learning organization, agile, lean,* and *purpose driven* don't quite seem to capture it; they are manifestations, not the core, of what is needed. *Unfear* nails it, and its principles point to the profound personal roots that any organizational transformation requires.

—**MONICA MCGURK**, Chief Global Growth Officer
of Kellogg Company

When we transform our response to fear—that most visceral and evolutionarily wired human emotion—we transform our orientation to life, how we conduct business, and the outcomes we are able to generate. We no longer fall into the trap of trading well-being for success. Gaurav and Mark have written a book that comes from their hearts and yet draws on their decades of work with leaders and organizations. They've produced a blueprint for creating unfear organizations—adaptive, resilient in the face of adversity, and able to generate extraordinary results while putting the well-being of the human beings who make up the organization at the very center. Having worked with them for many years, I can vouch that their approach delivers what it promises.

—**DOUG WIRTH**, CEO of Amida Care

I have great respect for Gaurav and Mark and the work they do, having partnered with them on several initiatives at Harlem United. Yet, with so many organizational culture change how-tos on the market, I have to admit that I was a little skeptical of what I could learn from *Unfear*. But within just a few pages, that skepticism melted away. In *Unfear*, Gaurav and Mark present a new paradigm for creating true, lasting individual and organizational change. By sharing their own life experiences and real-world examples of their work, they make this a very relatable read. They provide actionable and practical guidelines for an unfear transformation. If you wonder why all the work you've done—the surveys, focus groups, trainings, workshops, strategic plans, and so on—hasn't led to truly sustainable change despite your sincere commitment to creating that change, read *Unfear*. If you are committed to creating a conscious, sustainable transformation—for yourself, your team, and your organization—this book will help you achieve that.

—**JACQUELYN KILMER,** CEO of Harlem United

Gaurav and Mark offer us a powerful path to harmonize organizational performance with employee well-being by reengineering the inner life of an organization and its people. Kudos! You can't read this book without taking away some valuable lessons and practical tools on how to acknowledge and transcend the fears we experience, individually and collectively, in our workplaces. Written for organizational leaders who understand that, in the end, we are all human.

—**HITENDRA WADHWA,** Professor of Practice at Columbia Business School and founder of Mentora Institute

I have worked with Gaurav and Co-Creation Partners at critical growth points for myself and my organization. I was able to grow immensely as a leader in a short period of time, becoming more courageous, authentic, and connected to the people around me. *Unfear* captures the spirit of our work, seamlessly blending business and philosophy concepts and frameworks with profound personal stories. Read it! It will fundamentally change the way you relate to yourself—replacing stress and fear with an earnest belief in your infinite potential and a resolute desire to unleash as much of it as you possibly can.

—**NICK CHRISTMAN,** Senior Vice President of Product and Client Operations at Namely

In today's world, building resilient organizations and societies is key to sustained growth and happiness. A critical part of this process is reimagining and reframing your relationship with fear. *Unfear* presents practical, actionable ways to do this—to free the angel in the stone. This inspiring must-read will empower your journey from fear to unfear!

—**JYOTI RAI,** Managing Director of Global Human Resources at Moody's Corporation

In this book, Mark and Gaurav share their wisdom and learnings from more than two decades of working closely with teams and organizations. And they make a very compelling argument that a common cause of underperformance of individuals and organizations is personal and cultural fear. Overcoming fear to move from a victim mentality to an ownership mentality and from a knower mentality to a learner mentality is necessary for individuals and organizations to reach their potential and compete in this economy. Highly recommended!

—**GURU SETHUPATHY,** Managing Vice President and
Head of People Strategy and Analytics at Capital One

Gaurav and Mark boldly take on the hidden yet biggest inhibitor to sustainable change in organizations, our individual and collective experience of fear at work. *Unfear* helps us stop and consider how our own leadership behaviors lead to organizations full of judgment, mistrust, and division. It shows us a clear path out of this dysfunction, one that starts with us as individuals. This is a deeply engaging and thought-provoking read with practical ideas you can apply with your teams as well as in your personal life.

—**DALTON LI,** Head of Strategic Enablement
and Advancement at Vanguard

Fear is one of the biggest inhibitors of personal and professional happiness. In *Unfear*, Gaurav and Mark do an amazing job of defining the different facets of fear and explaining practices that one can undertake to experience sustained transformation. This is a supremely practical book that is filled with personal stories and examples from their professional experiences. The passion they have for helping others comes through very strongly. A life-changing book!

—**VENU KANNAN,** Head of Professional Services
for the Americas at UiPath

Unfear

Transform Your Organization
to Create Breakthrough Performance
~~and or~~ Employee Well-Being

Gaurav Bhatnagar
Mark Minukas

New York   Chicago   San Francisco   Athens   London   Madrid
Mexico City   Milan   New Delhi   Singapore   Sydney   Toronto

1 2 3 4 5 6 7 8 9   LCR   26 25 24 23 22 21

ISBN   978-1-264-26816-0
MHID   1-264-26816-5

e-ISBN   978-1-264-26817-7
e-MHID   1-264-26817-3

Library of Congress Cataloging-in-Publication Data

Names: Bhatnagar, Gaurav, author. | Minukas, Mark, author.
Title: Unfear : transform your organization to create breakthrough
   performance and employee well-being / Gaurav Bhatnagar and Mark Minukas.
Description: New York : McGraw Hill, [2022] | Includes bibliographical
   references and index.
Identifiers: LCCN 2021033748 (print) | LCCN 2021033749 (ebook) | ISBN
   9781264268160 (hardback) | ISBN 9781264268177 (ebook)
Subjects: LCSH: Organizational change. | Employee motivation. | Well-being.
   | Resilience (Personality trait)
Classification: LCC HD58.8 .B4962 2021 (print) | LCC HD58.8 (ebook) |
   DDC 658.4/06—dc23
LC record available at https://lccn.loc.gov/2021033748
LC ebook record available at https://lccn.loc.gov/2021033749

McGraw Hill books are available at special quantity discounts to use as premiums and sales promotions or for use in corporate training programs. To contact a representative, please visit the Contact Us pages at www.mhprofessional.com.

To the thousands who have traveled with us
on the unfear journey,
our greatest teachers and friends

Contents

unfear verb

\\'ən-fir\\

: to fundamentally shift your relationship with fear and use it as a cue for learning and growth

unfear noun

: a choice to develop self-mastery in the face of adversity

unfear adjective

: having or showing the ability to transform fear into opportunities for learning and growth

Foreword

When I first heard that Gaurav and Mark would call their book *Unfear*, the name struck an immediate chord. I've spent most of my career working for large, often successful organizations. At several of these stops, I've noticed how fear can pervade and corrode workplace culture and performance. At one company in particular, I felt the pain that too much fear can cause.

It was an outwardly successful company, and I had a fairly high position. Upper management relied, in part, on fear to drive performance. One of my colleagues, who didn't get along well with the divisional manager, suggested that the company conduct a buyout of part of our division. The executive committee for our division (on which we both sat and was chaired by our divisional manager) decided to proceed with the buyout.

Later, when I looked over the minutes of that executive meeting, I noticed that our discussion on the buyout had not been recorded. This struck me as strange, and I let my colleague know. I warned him to proceed with some caution. All the same, he contacted an investor about a potential buyout. It turned out, however, that our divisional manager never informed the CEO of the company. When the CEO found out, he was not amused. My colleague was fired on the spot.

It eventually became a court case, and my colleague asked if I would volunteer to testify on his behalf. Even though I felt the need to, I said that I wouldn't volunteer. I'd only go if called. I did this out of self-preservation. Looking back, I realize now that I had become caught up in the fear-based culture. I wanted to take a stand, but only in a way that wouldn't jeopardize my own advancement.

In the jurisdiction where this happened, witnesses could not be called. Instead, the divisional manager asked three of my colleagues on the executive committee for a signed statement claiming that we had never discussed a buyout. They all agreed. All this fear in the company made people willing to betray beloved colleagues. I decided I needed to either change this environment or leave it. So I started to speak up more.

Not long after, I was sacked as well.

This was painful for me and my family. But it was also one of the best things that ever happened to me. I felt free again to choose my own destiny. I decided that I wanted to lead organizations that deliver the best results in terms of employee, customer, and shareholder satisfaction. The most important word in that last short sentence is the word *and*. Let me share a bit more on this concept.

To me, a company needs to ensure that there is a safe environment where colleagues can speak up. Your title is less important than what you can contribute, and I consider it the responsibility of leaders to empower everyone else to make an impact.

When your teams are in a good place—when everyone trusts and supports each other—there is little fear. Your customers will notice this. I have seen that organizations with great employee and customer satisfaction deliver great results. Employee satisfaction, customer satisfaction, and shareholder satisfaction go hand in hand.

Gaurav and Mark understand this better than almost anybody I've met, and this book is a valuable addition to the cultural transformation world. Gaurav and Mark demystify fear in the workplace with their tremendous honesty. They speak bravely and eloquently about their own journeys and the journeys of people with whom they've worked. They blend their narrative with plenty of practical advice, but it is their deft personal touch that stands out. And it is that personal touch that I've seen Gaurav use so spectacularly in his workshops.

When I first started working with Gaurav, I saw the transformative potential that unfear has on employee performance. My colleagues and I invited Gaurav and a few other consultants to come in and work with us at our top-100 meeting at Unilabs, the leading European diagnostic company, where I currently serve as executive chairman. There Gaurav led us through some workshops where we combined a 360-degree review, in which an employee's boss, subordinates, and peers all provide feedback to that employee, with an iceberg session, during which we attempted to understand the motivations that led to the behaviors described in the feedback session.

By combining these two techniques, Gaurav was able to create a breakthrough for many of our employees. This sort of work can have tremendous power. In another setting, I saw it spur a huge transformation for one of my employees. He was a super successful director of sales. This was a large, extremely fit man, a very compelling and powerful presence. In the 360-degree feedback session, everyone talked about how much they appreciated the results that he got. He made lots of money for the company and had an excellent record in closing new clients. Yet many of his peers and subordinates also mentioned that he had a tendency to claim all the credit for himself. We suspected that this was connected to fear, so we asked him where this tendency came from.

He told a story about how, when he was a young child, his father took him and his younger brother to the beach. The father left the two boys alone to go and get some ice cream. In the five minutes that his father was gone, his younger brother drowned.

This experience had a profound impact on the life of the sales director. How could it not? He constantly felt this fear that he wasn't good enough, couldn't take good enough care of himself and his family. He felt a need to always prove himself. He became a champion swimmer in high school. This same wound, in some part, drove the ambition that made him so effective at sales. And it also led to his tendency to hog all the credit, which created friction with other members of his team.

Once he shared this story, it completely changed the dynamic between him and his team. He felt more comfortable sharing the credit, and the team felt better able to understand his motivations. It ultimately made them work better together and deliver even greater results. Gaurav and his team have a deep mastery of this sort of work. They get a full view and dig deep, and they help people understand how their fear holds them back.

When Gaurav asked me to write the Foreword to the book that he and Mark were about to publish, I was both honored and humbled. Honored, because he trusted me to be a small part of their ambition to publish this great book. More important, I felt humbled, because I know there is so much work for me to further unfear both in my organization and within myself. That is the beautiful, frustrating thing about any attempt to unfear: it is a never-ending process, one that will continually offer new challenges—and even greater rewards.

My wish for all of you is that this wonderful book by Gaurav and Mark will help you to unfear both on a personal level and on an organizational level. Remember, when you do what you fear, you kill the fear.

Jos Lamers
Executive Chairman of Unilabs

Acknowledgments

We are riding on the shoulders of giants whose teachings have shaped our thinking. We hope that we've combined and channeled these teachings in ways that are uniquely useful to business leaders in the world. We've been lucky to have been enveloped throughout our lives, professionally and personally, by caring and supportive people who have provided us with the space to express and refine our craft.

Shobha Nayar, coleader at Co-Creation Partners, your energy and initiative ensured that this book idea got off the ground. You provided us with structure, kept us honest to our commitments, and challenged our thinking throughout the writing process. Without you, this book would have remained a figment of our imagination.

Dylan Hoffman, our writing coach, you helped us find our collective voice and, with a great bedside manner, and endless patience for our unpredictable writing process, coached us to write a cogent narrative for which we all can be proud.

Casey Ebro, our editor at McGraw Hill, you believed in our core ideas, applied your sharp eye for detail, and gave us the opportunity to reach a larger audience than we could on our own.

Linda Konner, our agent, you were the first believer and our trusted guide through the unfamiliar terrain of publishing across geographies and platforms.

Robin Colucci, you helped us shape our initial ideas and masterfully guided us through the long and winding book creation process. Thank you for your initial spark of encouragement and steady guidance to us throughout.

The Co-Creation team, you are our innermost circle. We cannot thank you enough for your patience, cheerleading, and most important, courage to work with us on building an organization that dares to live what it preaches, even when it's difficult to do so.

Our clients, you have been our teachers, fellow co-creators, and close companions on the unfear journey. There would have been no journey and no book without you.

Our beta readers, you shared your precious time, candid feedback, and loving encouragement. We are blessed to have friends like you.

McKinsey & Co, thank you for providing the space for expansive learning, meaningful challenges, and connection to some incredibly special people.

Newfield Network and Julio Olalla, you expanded our view on coaching and gave us new contexts to incorporate into our own approach with clients.

From Gaurav

To the three sages whom I have been blessed to learn from:

- Gita Bellin, thank you for your light, wisdom, and Shiva arrows that opened the door and pulled me through.
- Michael Rennie, thank you for your charisma, insight, and role modeling that inspired me to aspire to be more than who I thought I could be.

- Swami Bodhananda, thank you for your joyous spirit and spiritual clarity and teaching that allowed me to get a glimpse into my true nature and, from that place, live a more unfear life.

From Mark

To some of the closest sages from whom I've been so lucky to learn:

- My parents, thank you for encouraging me to follow my own path in life and for your role modeling of acceptance, understanding, and love.
- Sarah, my wife, thank you for providing the psychological and physical space (mostly on weekends and holidays) for me to write this book, especially during a pandemic when space was hard to come by, and thank you for your example of facing fear with a learning mindset and doggedly following your deeply held values in life.
- Audra and Sirene, my girls, thank you for your everyday example of how to live in joy and the present moment—thank you for showing me, in the most visceral and genuine of ways, how to live in an unfear way.

Introduction

F ear is taboo in most organizations. To admit fear is to admit
weakness, failure, or that you can't handle the demands of your
job. Everybody ignores its existence. At the same time, organizations use fear to drive short-term performance. They ratchet up the pressure while pretending it's not part of the calculus.

The twenty-first century is off to a fear-inducing start. The number of
people with anxiety disorders has exploded. Everything from the climate
to the economy, the social fabric, political institutions, and even public
health seems less stable than it was in the 1980s and 1990s. The business
landscape is no different. It features a networked, hyperconnected, and
hypertransparent knowledge economy with ever-diminishing sources of
competitive advantage.

All this fear seeps into the very DNA of an organization. Once there,
it silently and insidiously drives dysfunction in every aspect of the organization: strategy, operations, cross-functional collaboration, human capital management, team dynamics, employee engagement, and employee
well-being. It's no wonder, then, that according to a recent McKinsey
Global Institute survey, only 30 percent of organizational transformation
efforts reach and sustain their top- and bottom-line goals.

This book is the antidote to the problem of fear.

First, the answer to fear is not a fear-free organization. *Fear itself is not the problem.* Humans are biologically wired to experience fear, and for good reason. It is vital to identifying and avoiding or addressing threats and ensuring our survival. Negating or ignoring fear can get us hurt or worse. But becoming overly fearful is detrimental to our growth and development. The solution is to *transform our relationship with fear.* Fear in itself is just an emotion, which is neither good nor bad. It is necessary to understand the underlying message beneath our fear and to make different, more positive choices in the face of that fear.

To get a sense of what we mean, consider this story that Geoff Mead shares in his book *Telling the Story:*[1]

Some years ago, a group of Bushmen agreed to lead a party of anthropologists into the Kalahari to see some ancient rock paintings that were rumored to be found deep in the desert. After two weeks, traveling through the sandy wastes, they came to an escarpment and the Bushmen announced that they had arrived.

The anthropologists took out their equipment and scoured the sacred site. They peeked and peered, they brushed and scraped but found nothing, not a single painting. After a while they gave up, complaining that they had been brought to the wrong place.

The Bushmen laughed and went up to the same spot that the anthropologists had so closely examined; they unstoppered the gourds of water they had with them and splashed the contents over the sun-bleached surface of the rock. Dozens of dazzling colored images—women, children, hunters, eland, kudu, wildebeest and lions—sprang from the rock and burst into life.

Those beautiful images are akin to the actions and choices that we can make that lead to breakthrough performance and employee well-being. They exist even when we cannot see them. And usually we cannot see them because we are blinded by fear. This is a common feature of fear—it usually highlights where we need to grow. Think about a time when you underwent significant growth in your life. At the start of that process, what did you feel? Fear? Anxiety? Trepidation? How did you initially move through that fear? Did you try to avoid it or suppress it? Or did you see the positive possibilities it may have revealed? Realizing that fear indicates an opportunity to grow is like throwing water on those sun-drenched rocks. Now, when we face our fears, instead of seeing only the potential for failure, we can see tremendous possibility.

Second, organizations need to turn traditional transformation theory on its head. We advocate for an *inside-out transformation*, one that starts with the mindsets of individuals, influences their behavior, and then impacts teams and finally the organization. Why? Because organizations don't transform—individuals do. And transformation begins at the level of mindsets. This is a radical shift in thinking. Typically, organizational transformation programs start with a focus on systems, processes, and structures before addressing individual behaviors . . . and possibly mindsets. This approach is rational, but it doesn't fundamentally address the ways in which fear operates in an organization. The result, although often positive, is less sustainable. The unfear solution requires comprehensive work on all three dimensions of organizational life—individuals, teams, and the organizational system—and the mindsets that operate at each of these levels.

Finally, *organizational performance and employee well-being are not mutually exclusive.* Both can exist simultaneously. From a fear-based perspective, these objectives live in tension. Leaders in many organizations believe, falsely, that they can *either* have an organization that performs exceptionally well at the expense of employee well-being *or* an organization that prioritizes employee well-being at the expense of high performance. In this book, we will show you the way to achieve *both* high performance *and* employee well-being by addressing how people relate to their fears individually and collectively.

This journey begins with seeing differently. As Marcel Proust said, "The real voyage of discovery consists not in seeking new landscapes, but in having new eyes." This book is meant to help you do just that.

We set out on our work to unfear because we are both, in our unique ways, recovering fear addicts. We have come to realize how fear sits at the root of many of the problems we see in business and the world at large, and we have dedicated our careers to unfearing ourselves and others.

I, Gaurav, used fear to motivate myself during the bulk of my 11 years at McKinsey and Company. It worked, in a way. I experienced success. But without even realizing it, I created a life of dysfunction and limited the performance of my teams. I mishandled relationships and people. In other words, I sabotaged myself. As you will read, I went through a profound experience when I was in McKinsey, South Africa, which became the basis of my work. The ideas and concepts in this book are drawn from my 20-year journey to unfear, experiencing incredible breakthroughs and a few breathtaking stumbles. Over that time, I gained mastery in helping people understand and shift their mindsets in order to improve their own performance. Yet I struggled to create systemic change within organizations. It wasn't until I met Mark, with his expertise in business operations and systems, that together we were able to create a truly holistic unfear program.

I, Mark, have devoted my career over the last 22 years to learning how complex organizational systems operate and how they can be improved. I studied systems and human factors engineering and learned that the root cause for the failure of most systems wasn't bad engineering but rather human factors. At each stop in my career since—as a civil engineer and Seabee (a play on C and B, which stand for "Construction Battalion") in the Navy and later as a management consultant, I discovered just how often human factors sabotage systems. I often took an engineering approach to problems, attempting to find the right answer, but I consistently failed to achieve the results I wanted. Eventually, I realized that having the "right" answer and designing the most beautiful systems were completely worthless if you couldn't get other people to buy in, if you didn't pair it with culture change. After meeting Gaurav, I developed strategies to apply systematic change and transformation in a way that simultaneously helps to unfear an organization and to power an overall cultural transformation that creates breakthrough performance and well-being.

Combined, we have spent 150,000 hours in pursuit of unfear. Together we have facilitated the unfear transformations of more than 1,000 business leaders and hundreds of organizations to unleash both performance and well-being.

This book is divided into two parts. Part I (Chapters 1–3) explores fear—its impact, its biological underpinnings, and the archetypes through which it is expressed as patterns of behavior in organizations. We'll be spending time in the belly of the beast.

Part II (Chapters 4–8) explores unfear. We talk about the benefits and lay out some guidelines about how to bring about an unfear transformation. It is hardly an exhaustive list, nor is it a step-by-step process. Rather, we show you a destination and how you might get there. We offer strategies, techniques, and actions you can take. You may use them or come up with your own. What matters is that you embark on the journey from fear to unfear because it's ultimately the better choice for yourself, your team, and your organization.

As with any journey, you will experience both highs and lows, epiphanies and frustrations, challenges and insights. Just when you think you have it figured out, you may be provoked by a story, an idea, or a construct. As you read, reflect on the questions at the end of each chapter, and be honest about yourself and your organization. If you are challenged or upset by a story or concept, give yourself the luxury of time to understand what it presents to you. When you have an insight, take the opportunity to clarify how you will act on it. If you are lost or have a question, feel free to reach out to us at gauravandmark@unfearbook.com. If you'd like to be part of a community that is traveling this journey together, visit www.unfearbook.com and sign up.

We hope that you experience as much learning and growth from reading this book as we did in writing it. We look forward to hearing from you to continue the dialogue and build on the ideas we have shared. Let's keep learning together.

Part I
FEAR

Part 7

PLATE

1

Fear and Unfear

Unfear is not the opposite of fear, nor is it a synonym for *fearless*. To *unfear* is to reframe the experience of fear so that we can make different choices in response. It means shifting the story we carry within us about fear and seeing the learning that fear offers us. In the chapters that follow we will show you that this reframing is possible, and we will provide you with powerful ideas and practices on how to make this reframing a natural state of being for yourself and your organization.

We do not promise that this will be easy, but we do promise that if you and your organization go through this transformation, your organization will have built a powerful learning system that will be able to face any business challenge with agility and courage, and you will have a vibrant organization in which personal joy and business performance flourish together.

The unfear process of reframing will free you from your reactive patterns to fear and allow you to be in mastery rather than having fear control you. It will enable a state of being in which you welcome fear as an opportunity to learn, a state that unlocks sustained high performance as an individual, a team, and an organization.

However, before we examine the unfear process, let's understand how fear works in us and the impact it has on us and our organizations.

> *The unfear process will enable a state of being in which you welcome fear as an opportunity to learn, a state that unlocks sustained high performance as an individual, a team, and an organization.*

Fear

People google "fear" more than 100,000 times a week. Fear sits prominently at the forefront of most of our minds. In our work on strategy, culture, and operations over the past 20 years, we have discovered that fear is the single biggest source of waste in organizations today. At the same time, it is the least understood, most neglected, and most dramatically underestimated issue in modern organizational life.

Whenever we start a transformation effort with a new organization, we can feel the tension in all the participants as they file into the first workshop. They have no idea what to expect and have no sense that by the end of the process they will know how fear has driven their lives and kept them shackled to suboptimal behaviors. When they see the chairs arranged in a semicircle, they mumble to each other, laugh nervously, and make jokes about being in an Alcoholics Anonymous meeting.

Over the course of our work, we slow things down and create space for everyone, from CEOs down to frontline workers, to reflect in a whole different way. As the tension fades and participants feel safe, the real stories begin to emerge. People realize, many for the first time, that they are not the only ones in the organization feeling afraid and that, finally, they can have the real conversations needed to build a healthier and high-performing organization.

> *Fear is the single biggest source of waste in organizations today. At the same time, it is the least understood, most neglected, and most dramatically underestimated issue in modern organizational life.*

While most of us believe that we know what fear is, we don't fully understand the different ways in which it affects our thoughts, actions, and ultimately the results we realize. While the technical definition of fear is "an unpleasant emotion caused by the belief that someone or something is dangerous, likely to cause pain, or a threat,"[1] it takes many different forms in our minds. The things we perceive as dangerous are so diverse, personal, and ingrained in us that we might not even recognize them as threats. We just feel a sense of generalized stress. Often, when people articulate their fears to us, it's the first time that they understand their experience of stress is rooted in fear.

In our work with organizations, we have seen fear manifest in countless forms, but some of the most common are:

- Fear of a boss who is verbally abusive
- Fear of losing a job
- Fear of asserting oneself or speaking up
- Fear of pushing back on unreasonable expectations
- Fear of public speaking
- Fear of asking for a promotion
- Fear of sharing new ideas
- Fear of being shut down
- Fear of being undermined by a coworker
- Fear of being an imposter
- Fear of not belonging
- Fear of being lonely
- Fear of "staying stuck"

- Fear of change
- Fear of being adventurous
- Fear of failure

We have never encountered a single person who had no fears. Yet, magically, whenever we meet senior business leaders in their corporate boardrooms, they never talk about how fear hinders performance. They never acknowledge the fear-based patterns that drive corporate strategy, personnel decisions, organizational politics, collaboration, operational decisions, and the creation of dense, multilevel bureaucracies.

There are three main reasons why the negative impact of fear remains unexamined:

1. **You can't manage what you can't measure.** Many leaders pick up this utilitarian management theory in business school. It is difficult to directly measure the impact of fear (or any other emotion) on performance, so managers often ignore it altogether.

2. **Taboos around fear.** Many leaders view admitting to fear as a sign of weakness, as being soft and touchy-feely, which doesn't align with the current paradigm of strong, decisive leadership. Others see fear in the organization as an indictment of their capability, so they either pretend it doesn't exist or give excuses for why it does.

3. **Fear drives short-term performance.** Because fear works in the short term, few leaders stop to question the potential damage that it is doing over the long term. Indeed, they might even believe that fear is necessary. We've met countless executives who say that they need to use fear to drive their teams—that without clear incentive structures and punishments, their employees won't work as hard as the organization requires. Many large organizations create hypercompetitive structures in an attempt to filter out the people who can't handle them. A classic example of this is "rank-and-yank," a management philosophy first popularized by Jack Welch,

the legendary CEO of GE. Every year GE ranked each employee against his or her peers and fired those in the bottom 10 percent. Organizations such as Amazon, IBM, and Microsoft have all used some version of this process. We can't deny that it gets results—those are three of the most profitable organizations in history, and Welch led GE to its most profitable years. These fear-based programs, however, only work in limited ways. They can improve profits and shareholder value in the short term but completely neglect the cost to organizational effectiveness and employee well-being in the long term.

Making the Invisible Visible

To unfear, you must first recognize fear and how it might be impacting how you, your teams, and your organization behave. There are three key aspects about fear to understand:

- Where it comes from
- How we (try to) deal with it
- Its long-term impacts

Where Fear Comes From

No human will ever fully escape fear. It is intrinsically linked to our survival. To eliminate fear, to be fearless, would mean completely denying our nature. Likewise, no organization will ever escape fear. An organization is nothing but an amalgamation of people working together. The only way to remove fear from an organization would be to remove the people as well. That said, there are two factors in our contemporary reality that make modern organizations particularly powerful hotbeds of fear.

Increasing Volatility. Human beings yearn for certainty, even at the expense of other comforts. A 2016 study from University College, London[2] showed that participants experienced greater stress when they had a 50 percent chance of receiving an electric shock than when they had a 100 percent chance. In other words, they felt less fear when facing a more negative but certain outcome. However, we live in a world of increasing volatility, uncertainty, complexity, and ambiguity. The accelerated pace at which organizations must respond to change induces deep fear—about profits, competition, job security, income, and mobility—for the CEO and frontline workers alike.

Short-Termism. This style of thinking is most obviously prevalent in large, publicly traded organizations. Toward the end of the twentieth century, companies gradually prioritized shareholder value to the detriment of all other stakeholders. As a result, organizations focus more on profits than on creating value for consumers, employees, and communities. They plan for shorter and shorter terms, focusing on generating more impressive quarterly numbers. All of this puts extra pressure and stress on every individual in the company.

Our point is not to pass a value judgment on shareholder primacy, just that fear, anxiety, and stress are by-products of this metric. Organizations that ignore this reality slap a veneer of normalcy on an inherently unhealthy system. They ignore the constant, self-perpetuating breakdowns in human interactions that come from the fear they create.

Short-termism is by no means limited to publicly traded companies. It's evident in private enterprises where leaders prioritize profits and short-term survival at the expense of investments (in new hires and training) that will create longer-term, but perhaps less certain, success. A similar dynamic plays out in the nonprofit world, where organizations in a budget crunch prioritize what will allow them to scrape by today instead of making investments that will keep them relevant in the future. This mindset even pops up in government organizations, which experience a high degree of turnover in the upper ranks (which correspond to election cycles). New leaders think they need to make a quick impact, so they might make changes just for change's sake. The employees, many of whom will outlast the leader, display short-term thinking by resisting the changes. They believe that they can just wait out a boss whom they don't like. At the end of the day, neither the leader nor the employees can move past this short-term mindset to build something lasting.

Our Current Approaches to Fear

Typically, an organization takes one of three failing approaches to fear. They ignore it, try to reduce it with overly simplistic solutions, or use it as a driver of performance. Ignoring fear obviously doesn't work, but it's worth examining why the other two responses are equally, if not more, dysfunctional.

Overly Simplistic Solutions. When organizations undertake fear-reduction efforts, they tend to prescribe overly simplistic solutions to complicated problems. While each effort is unique in its own way, we see two common patterns that hold these efforts back.

The first is to take *too limited of a view of fear*. Most "psychological safety" initiatives in organizations only address fears that are readily obvious in an organizational context, such as fear of challenging a boss, sharing criticism, and so on. Psychological safety and the recent rush to implement it come from Professor Amy Edmondson's bestselling book, *The Fearless Organization*.[3] Edmondson has a compelling and useful perspective on fear in the workplace. But often, when people take up a psychological safety effort, they do so with a very rudimentary understanding of Edmondson's work and of fear in general. What they don't understand is that those surface-level fears listed earlier are just the symptoms of a deeper fear. That deeper, motivating fear might be a fear of failure, of rejection, of not being smart enough, of not being accepted, of not being loved, and so on. To really address fear in the workplace, to reshape the conversation around fear and eliminate dysfunction, you need to dig deeper and help people understand and address their underlying fears. If you don't, the smaller, symptomatic fears will keep popping up, no matter how much you invest in organizational psychological safety.

The second pattern involves *leaders who don't understand how their actions drive fear in an organization*. For example, one of our clients, a financial services organization, asked us to help with a culture and operational transformation effort. The new CEO realized that the organization did not engage in open dialogue about problems and that employees didn't challenge senior leaders enough. He suspected that this all led to suboptimal decision-making and performance. To reduce interpersonal fear and improve dialogue, the CEO started building a psychologically safe work environment. Before the psychological safety initiative even had a chance to succeed, some key investors advised the CEO that his cost base was too high. Senior leadership then started a head-count reduction that ran parallel to the psychological safety initiative. This head-count reduction, of course, made several employees terrified that they would lose their jobs.

The CEO didn't think that his actions were contradictory at all. He thought that psychological safety was about reducing fear of having open dialogue and that head-count reduction was about right-sizing the organization and achieving financial outcomes. He saw no link between the two initiatives. Although the CEO's decision made rational sense—he needed to reduce costs and improve effectiveness—fear has nothing to do with rationality. Human beings do not compartmentalize their fears. Anxiety about job security inevitably bleeds into fears about interpersonal communication.

> *Human beings do not compartmentalize their fears.*

Unsurprisingly, employees started feeling doubly unsafe because of these actions. People developed a deep suspicion of the management team. They felt that management was talking from both sides of their mouth. This story underscores why it is impossible to create a *fearless* culture while making the difficult decisions necessary to run a business. Fear will always exist. The question is how you engage with it.

Using Fear to Drive Short-Term Performance. The other common choice that people make is to use fear to drive performance. This is probably the greatest and trickiest issue with fear. While fear can lead to short-term results, it inevitably leads to significant dysfunction, underperformance, and waste in the long term. Take, for example, one of our clients, a factory located in the southern United States, which had teetered on the brink of failure for a decade. Eventually, the parent company, a global manufacturing organization, ran the numbers and concluded that with some savvy management, the plant could run profitably again. The parent company asked the plant manager, a successful leader with over 20 years of experience whom we'll call "John," to right-size the organization. In other words, let go 250 employees. John's first response was a mental, "Oh, shit," and a spike of fear that if he did not fix things, the entire organization—and his job—would be in jeopardy. Still in the throes of that initial spike of fear, he instructed his team to identify people to cut from the workforce. At the same time, he created a thermometer graphic, with "0" at the bottom and "250" at the top, and every time he let someone go, he added another notch to the thermometer. The thermometer was on display at every presentation he gave and at every meeting he held. His leadership paradigm was to use fear to spark his team to make difficult decisions they might otherwise try to avoid.

While John got an immediate reduction of 20 full-time employees, his own fear-based response created a lot of fear in the organization. Imagine going to work with this thermometer dangling over your head, reminding you that people were being let go and that you might very well be next! How would that make you feel? What might you do? Work harder, yes. But you might also compete with fellow employees and try to undermine them. You might get frustrated and work to sabotage management. You might just go with the flow, even when you do not agree with what's going on.

This made John's problem worse, and he doubled down by applying more pressure, which led to more of the same negative behaviors from the staff. In this death spiral, the more John tried, the deeper the hole became. (We'll come back to John later in this chapter.)

The Long-Term Impact of Fear

John isn't alone in his approach. Many leaders use fear to drive short-term performance and hope that they can use their position, charm, or both to manage the fallout. More often than not, they're wrong. The fear in these organizations remains radioactive and, over the long term, negatively impacts performance and well-being at three different levels: the individual, the team, and the organization.

On Individual Performance and Well-Being. Shaquille O'Neal tells a story about trying to convince a young Kobe Bryant to pass the ball and saying to him, "There is no I in team."

Kobe replied, "Sure, but there's an M and an E in that m***erf***r."

While Kobe probably said this because he was afraid that his teammates couldn't support him, he does touch on an important point about the nature of teams and organizations: the individual is the basic building block and most precious resource of an organization. Yet fear mishandles this resource because it prevents people from fully expressing their innate potential. Fearful employees usually don't say no to their managers, push back, or offer their own ideas. They just get on with the work. For many years, organizations considered this model behavior. But in the volatility of today's information economy, companies need employees who respond to complexity and uncertainty with passion, creativity, and resilience. And they cannot do this when they are afraid.

Early in our careers, we both dealt with the negative impact of fear.

I (Mark) let fear detract from my performance. As a hypercompetitive person, I've always struggled with admitting that I don't know something and asking for help. As someone drawn to math and science and who studied engineering, I learned to believe that there was only one right answer to problems and that smart, capable people should find that answer for themselves. At the same time, I was insecure and terrified of failure and rejection. Together these fears and beliefs created several dysfunctional patterns for me.

Early in my career as a diver and officer in the U.S. Navy, I was involved in a military exercise off the coast of southern California. The Navy has these big barges that can be sunk a little way off shore and that can pump water and fuel to personnel carrying out operations on shore. They are essentially mobile gas stations, and my team members and I were practicing the setup and operation of one of these barges in case we ever needed to deploy one. I was the most junior diver and had to wait all week to take my first dive. Right before the exercise was finished, I got a chance. The master diver gave me some quick instructions about what to do, and I donned my hardhat diving equipment and entered the water. Then, 120 feet down, I looked at all the valves on the barge and realized that I didn't know what to do. I had no idea which valves to open and which to close. I was new to that line of work, and because of the nitrogen gas building up in my veins from the dive, I was feeling almost drunk.

At this point, I could have easily used my "umbilical cord"—the reinforced air tube and communication wire that tethered me to the boat—to tell the master diver that I didn't know what to do. I didn't. My fear of being judged by others kept me from taking that step. I took an educated guess on which valves to open—one that proved wrong. Luckily, nothing I did created a safety hazard. It slowed down the whole operation, people had to dive again to fix my mistakes, and I got stuck with the nickname "Righty Tighty, Lefty Loosey" because of my gaffe.

The nickname wasn't the only thing that stuck—I couldn't drop the habit of not asking for help. When I left the military to work as a consultant, I often faced situations where I needed assistance but didn't ask for it. My stubborn self-sufficiency also prevented me from cultivating mentors during my early years at McKinsey. I believed that I had to struggle through difficult situations on my own to get "full credit." By not asking for help, though, I simply made my life more difficult, and after a few years, I felt incredibly isolated and alone. My attempt to win through my own heroic efforts all but ensured less than optimal performance.

I (Gaurav) can relate, but in a slightly different way. When I was a junior consultant, fear significantly impacted my well-being more than it did my performance. I was an insecure overachiever, hypercompetitive and obsessed with achieving merely for the sake of achieving. I took great pride in the fact that the acceptance rate at the business school I went to was less than 0.21 percent. I only worked for McKinsey because the firm hadn't hired me right out of business school, and I felt vindicated by the fact that they eventually wanted me. I was obsessed with checking the next box and pushed myself as hard as I could. I slept only two or three hours a night, using the firm's car service to get to the office by four o'clock most mornings. I spent almost no time with my two young kids, and my marriage was a disaster. I didn't exercise, and my diet was terrible. Even though my performance was fine, I felt miserable.

I knew, on some intuitive level, that my relationship with fear was harming my health and happiness. Those suspicions were confirmed when I came across a book called *Feel the Fear and Do It Anyway*, by Susan Jeffers.[4] Reading it made me recognize the unsustainable, destructive path I'd gone down. But I was still stuck in fear. I felt like being caught with a self-help book about fear would destroy my carefully crafted image as a hard-charging, no-BS McKinsey consultant. I read *Feel the Fear* on the sly—in my hotel room late at night, when I was alone on flights, and during the few hours I spent at home.

Early in our careers, we both operated from and were motivated by deeply held fears—of not being enough, of losing, of letting people in our lives down, of looking foolish. Whenever individuals operate from one of these deeply held fears, they fall into one of two common patterns (which we discuss at length later in this book): a *Passive/Defensive pattern*, in which they hold back their ideas, not challenge the status quo, and wait to be directed rather than take the initiative, or an *Aggressive/Defensive pattern*, in which they take action through a win-lose paradigm and consider asking for help a sign of weakness. While you might think that one is more productive than the other, the truth is that both have dramatic negative effects on individual performance and well-being.

On Team Performance and Well-Being. Whenever we ask our clients to recall a time when they were part of a high-performing team, they usually tell stories about intense, hard-working environments where team members frequently had constructive debates about different ideas and ways to move forward. They talk about groups that didn't let relationship conflict or stress get in the way of their work and situations in which they could have honest disagreements with their colleagues without any fear that the colleague would take their comments personally. In short, they describe a team that could effectively engage in challenging conversations about performance, attitude, alignment, direction, and strategy. These conversations promote well-being within a team. If team members feel that they can't address an issue with their colleagues, they will suppress their emotions, obsess over them, and let them fester and grow. This poisons team members, creates unproductive stress, and makes it more likely for work to impact them when they get home because they can't process and let go of whatever is bothering them. Alternatively, they might have that difficult conversation, but in a clumsy, aggressive manner. When they do that, they merely spread the poison to the rest of the team.

We discuss how to effectively have these conversations later in this book, but for now, it's enough to know that these conversations depend on trust. When there is too much fear in a team—either between colleagues (i.e., one person is afraid of another) or within oneself (i.e., I'm afraid that I will fail)—it completely destroys trust. The good news about trust and difficult conversations is that they create a virtuous cycle, a positive-feedback loop, whereby difficult conversations build trust, and the more trust there is within a team, the more effective it becomes at difficult conversations.

Teams that operate on fear prevent these conversations from taking place. For example, we once worked with the leadership team of a global leader in healthcare. Even though the company was a leader, its revenue was stalling, and the board didn't like the company's prognosis. The board hired a new CEO, who was a turnaround specialist, to help get the company back on track. Right after becoming CEO, he implemented a series of unilateral actions and replaced almost 70 percent of the leadership team. If something went wrong in any department, he would fire its leader immediately. In doing so, he created a culture in which the leadership team couldn't make any decisions without his direct approval.

> *The good news about trust and difficult conversations is that they create a virtuous cycle, a positive-feedback loop, whereby difficult conversations build trust, and the more trust there is within a team, the more effective it becomes at difficult conversations.*

In fear for their jobs, nobody questioned the CEO or offered new ideas for improvement (in other words, they didn't have any difficult conversations). The senior leaders didn't trust the CEO to have their backs if a risk didn't pan out, so nobody took any risks. In the short run, everyone worked so hard that the CEO managed to turn the company around. He took this as proof of concept and became more entrenched in his way of operating. As time went on, because nobody engaged in difficult conversations, the business stagnated again. This only confirmed the CEO's belief that he couldn't depend on his team, so he drove them even harder. He started speaking negatively about his team members behind their backs, leading to an even greater breakdown of trust. This pulled the team and the entire organization into a downward spiral. It gummed up decision-making, created silos, and resulted in costly strategic mistakes. The CEO felt a great degree of fear and pressure to turn the organization around and pushed that down the corporate ladder. Eventually, it hurt performance so much that, as we write this, the board is considering letting the CEO go.

We call this pattern the CEO fell into "the vicious fear cycle," where someone reacts to a perceived threat with aggression or apathy, which lowers the degree of trust within the organization and makes it more likely for others to take the same approach (Figure 1.1). The cycle often goes unnoticed because the aggressive/apathetic responses work in the short term. But they erode results over time. However, when we unfear, we flip this cycle. *Threats* become *opportunities for learning and growth*, the team has effective difficult conversations, and this bolsters trust and leads to more effective conversations in the face of new cues for learning.

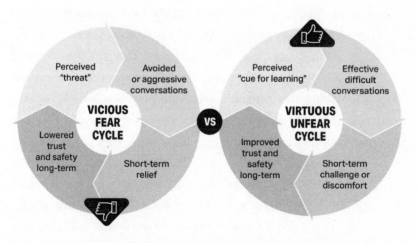

FIGURE 1.1   Vicious fear cycle versus virtuous unfear cycle

On Organizational Performance and Well-Being. Over a long-enough period of time, fear that causes individuals and teams to show up in a less-than-ideal way will eventually show up in a company's bottom line.

There are three primary reasons this happens: (1) fear leads to poor long-term strategy, (2) fear creates an environment that prevents a company from developing an inclusive, diverse culture, and (3) fear massively reduces employee engagement.

Poor Long-Term Strategy. When organizations and business leaders are in the throes of fear, they engage in a range of reactive responses that are ineffective. Some common reactive choices include:

- **Burying your head in the sand.** Organizations avoid acknowledging adversity and hope that it will go away. Traditional car manufacturers did this in response to the disruption created by Tesla. When Tesla came into the market, traditional manufacturers dismissed it as a sideshow and invented countless arguments on why the electric motor would never replace the combustion engine. In 2021, Tesla's market capitalization was $710.08 billion, which was larger than the next top five car makers—Toyota, Volkswagen, Daimler, General Motors, and Build Your Dreams (BYD)—*combined.*
- **Throwing money at the problem.** When business leaders do this, they are trying to find solutions before they really understand the problem. They never take the time to question the mindset or thinking that actually caused the problem, instead burning through cash to solve the issue as it appears on the surface. One of the furnaces that companies pitch the most money into is digital transformation. According to the International Data Corporation, global spending on digital transformation will reach about $2.3 trillion in 2023.[5] Yet a 2020 Boston Consulting Group (BCG) study[6] shows that 70 percent of digital transformations fail to produce their desired objective. According to the study, the determining factor in their success or failure is the "people dimension,"[7] stating that "organizational inertia from deeply rooted behaviors is a big impediment."[8] In our experience, this inertia comes from a dysfunctional relationship with fear.

- **Cutting heads.** Leaders often see head-count reductions as a silver bullet to deliver cost savings. Yet, as Richard Barrett shows in his book, *Liberating the Corporate Soul*,[9] fewer than half the companies engaging in such reengineering efforts see an improvement in short-term profit and fewer than a third see productivity improvement. The reason so many of these change efforts fail to produce the desired effect is that management doesn't understand and acknowledge the fear these efforts create. The fear generated by poorly handled layoffs tears at the social fabric of a company, sabotages trust, and diminishes collective productivity and creativity.

- **Making a flashy acquisition.** Often, when a large organization fears that it lacks the capacity for innovation, it tries to solve the problem by buying a radical, forward-thinking, young firm. The senior leaders of the acquiring company, often out of fear that they will lose their jobs to the partners at the acquired firm, work so hard to assimilate the new firm that they destroy what made it unique and radical in the first place.

- **Starting a flavor-of-the-month transformation effort.** Usually these are the pet projects of leaders in an organization. They aren't necessarily large-scale investments, nor do they require head-count reductions. Almost every new leader's first move is to reorganize the company/division/team/etc. They come in and say, "The old system didn't work, so we will do this instead." But, of course, because there is no perfect system, the new system creates new problems while solving others. When this happens, many leaders fall down the transformation effort rabbit hole and start trying new management techniques, hoping to find one that will solve all their problems. For example, a global consumer goods manufacturer wanted to increase collaboration between its regional offices and its core functions. The company was organized around the core functions, so managers thought that they could solve the problem by creating a mix of the functions and the regional centers. That, however, didn't work because suddenly it was no longer clear who had decision-making power in terms of new-product development and strategy. It also became less clear who would get credit. If sales improved in India, would that be because the sales teams had figured something out or because the leaders in the Indian offices figured something out? This uncertainty led to a high amount of waste, internal jockeying for credit, and distrust. All of this slowed the innovation pipeline and created more fear. Leadership then decided that the answer to their problems would be a transformation to improve innovation, so they brought in an Agile expert. Leadership kept cycling through new organizational systems, ignoring the factor that caused each transformation effort to fail—fear. Worse, in creating constant uncertainty, they drove up the fear quotient even further.

Suboptimal Conversations on Diversity, Equity, and Inclusion. Greater diversity, equity, and inclusion (DEI) are not just moral imperatives, they also carry significant utilitarian benefits. A study by McKinsey & Company and the Society for Human Research Management (SHRM) evaluated the performance of organizations with different levels of workplace diversity. The study found that organizations that exhibit gender and ethnic diversity are, respectively, 15 and 35 percent more likely to outperform less diverse organizations.[10] And yet many organizations struggle with this issue. In private conversations with us, senior leaders from several organizations across industries acknowledged that employees often view discussions of DEI as a minefield. We've heard that people of color are weary of these conversations because far too often they only result in someone saying something that opens an old wound, whereas workers from more privileged backgrounds are afraid to engage because they don't want to make a mistake and say the wrong thing. As a result, people either never have these conversations or only engage in them superficially. A standard vocabulary around diversity and inclusion has spread throughout many large corporations, and it is far too easy for people to parrot these buzzwords without making any real changes to how they see the world and behave within it.

It's important to understand that having these conversations in a way that can create real change requires a tremendous amount of vulnerability—on all sides. It takes great skill in managing your own fear to have open conversations on difficult topics, to listen deeply to others, to empathize, and to understand the underlying fears and humanity we all share.

Lackluster Employee Engagement. As a valuation expert and collaborative consultant, David Bookbinder writes in *The New ROI: Return on Individuals*, "The value of a business is a function of how well the financial capital and the intellectual capital are managed by the human capital. You'd better get the human capital part right."[11] To get the most out of the human capital, you need employees to be engaged enough to put in discretionary effort: to go above and beyond their job descriptions, to find ways to improve their processes, and to bring all their creativity to work with them. When there is a great deal of fear in an organization, especially interpersonal fear, employees put in far less discretionary effort. Rather than leaning into difficult situations, employees lean back and wait for someone else to make decisions and act.

Unfear

Unfear is not about eliminating fear. Even if this were possible, it would be counterproductive. The goal is to shift the story we carry within us about fear and to see the opportunity for learning and growth that fear offers us as an individual, a team, and an organization. Accomplishing this shift results in a dramatically different organization—an *unfear organization*.

Traits of an Unfear Organization

Unfear organizations operate differently from traditional fear-based organizations. They are primed to embrace and lead today's highly networked, complex, and volatile knowledge economy. Here are the four most important traits that propel breakthrough performance and employee well-being:

1. **Continuous learning and systems thinking.** Unfear organizations emphasize systems thinking and continuous improvement instead of working to avoid errors. They encourage everyone to find and address the root causes of problems instead of relying on Band-Aid solutions. They support all employees in their growth and development and encourage them to work to their full potential. Unfear organizations are highly adaptive and are able to innovate to meet business challenges.

2. **Self-confidence.** Unfear organizations demonstrate self-confidence instead of the hubris or apathy that is common in traditional fear-based organizations. This impacts their thinking and decision-making in three main ways:

   a. When faced with a challenging situation, they reflect before making a decision instead of engaging in knee-jerk reactions. They stay in the discomfort of uncertainty to allow more creative solutions to emerge. In *Thinking, Fast and Slow*,[12] Daniel Kahneman and Amos Tversky describe this as "System 2 thinking," which is more thoughtful and more reflective than "System 1 thinking," which is quick and relies on shortcuts to make decisions.

   b. People in unfear organizations are willing to demonstrate vulnerability. This allows them to connect on a more human level and learn from each other, unlike insecure leaders who view vulnerability as weakness, attempt to control everything, and hold themselves apart from the group.

c. People in unfear organizations have the courage to say, "I don't know." They don't use this phrase to quit but rather to acknowledge that they have more to learn and then to attempt to learn it. They have the confidence to understand that not knowing is the first step on the path to learning and continuous growth.

3. **Commitment.** Unfear organizations don't rely on coercion to achieve stretch outcomes. Instead, they foster commitment. They inspire individuals and teams to go beyond their job descriptions. They recognize that commitment builds openness to future action, whereas coercion builds resistance. Commitment leads to high levels of motivation, engagement, and employee satisfaction.

4. **Radical candor.** Unfear organizations overcome the false dichotomy between caring about people and challenging them to improve performance. They do this through what CEO coach Kim Scott calls "radical candor,"[13] the ability to provide feedback and coaching from a place of deep care for the development of the person receiving the message. This practice allows people to know each other as humans not just as roles, which helps build high-performing teams that work with energy toward a collective and meaningful purpose.

While these are the most important, the traits of an unfear organization are functionally limitless. Table 1.1 illustrates the difference between a fear-based organization and an unfear organization.

> *Unfear is not about eliminating fear. The goal is to shift the story we carry within us about fear and to see the opportunity for learning and growth that fear offers us as an individual, a team, and an organization.*

TABLE 1.1   Traditional Organizations Versus Unfear Organizations

TRADITIONAL FEAR-BASED ORGANIZATION	UNFEAR ORGANIZATION
Purely driven by profit	Driven by creating value for all stakeholders (including profit)
Command and control; top down	Inclusive, leveraging insights from all parties
Parent-child orientation	Adult-adult orientation
Technical/process orientation	Adaptive *and* process orientation
Risk minimization	Healthy risk appetite
Efficiency focus	Effectiveness and efficiency focused
Either/or mindset	And mindset
Victim and blame orientation	Mastery orientation
Knower and expert mindset	Learner and curiosity mindset
Problem focused	Solution focused
Dysfunctional conflict	Creative conflict
Best practice oriented	Next practice oriented
Humans as resources	Humans as humans
Profile consistency in leaders	Diversity in leadership profile
Certainty and order	Chaordic—chaos within order

Reframing Fear

How do we change the narratives we hold around fear so that we can create an unfear transformation? To understand how this works, let's go back to John, his chemical plant, and his head-count reduction thermometer. When we saw the thermometer, we had to say, "John, this is just the most depressing thing we've ever seen."

His response was, "What do you expect me to do?" John believed that he had to choose between two awful options. He could either use fear to force short-term actions to increase profits or he could foster a nice, calm working environment that would ultimately fail and result in even larger job losses at the plant and likely cost him his job. For John, this was not much of a choice.

His fear motivated him to react aggressively, making draconian cuts. What John didn't expect was that this would create a whole host of other problems. Suddenly, all the employees were desperate to not be one of the 250 who lost their jobs. So they started either directly competing with or sabotaging one another or lying low, avoiding making big mistakes, and just trying to survive the slew of cuts. All these behaviors reduced the overall productivity of the plant. The more John tried, the worse the problem became.

We told John that the answer to his problem wasn't more fear—it was to unfear himself, his team, and his organization. In other words, he needed to reframe his relationship with fear and the relationship of everyone in the organization with fear so that they could make more empowered and creative choices. Instead of thinking, "I can *either* be feared and successful *or* loved and a failure," we encouraged John to ask, "Despite this current business challenge, how can I create a resilient culture that generates *both* high performance *and* employee well-being?"

Then we helped John build such a culture. We focused on enabling everyone involved—from executives to frontline workers—to create a new narrative around the layoffs. Through a process that involved several experiential, self-discovery workshops and practical hands-on working sessions, we shifted the typical parent-child dynamic that exists between management and employees to adult-to-adult engagement. We asked the employees to share their experiences at the factory. They talked about what the factory meant to them and what it meant to the town. They shared their anxieties about losing their jobs, and we encouraged management to share the pain they felt at having to let go of 250 employees. This is a vital part of unfearing the organization: simply acknowledging the fear and the pain inherent in these types of decisions. It allows members of an organization to view each other as humans as opposed to just roles, and to a certain extent it destigmatizes the fear that everybody feels. It also allows people to see the stories they have created about themselves and others and to recognize that they have *a choice* to reframe these stories to create different outcomes.

Over the course of the work, we discovered that the factory had been a key part of the community for decades. Some workers had family members from three generations employed at the site. In this small town, the factory was the major employer, and its influence stretched into other sectors of life. Nobody wanted to see the factory disappear.

We helped everyone connect with the essence of why they were there, and together with management and the employees as equal human beings, we reframed the layoffs. They moved beyond seeing the layoffs as a sign of corporate greed or as a decree handed down by distant overlords to recognizing that downsizing was really, as John put it, "the best option in a less-than-ideal situation"—an attempt to make sure that the factory did what it needed to do to thrive in the long run. This wasn't a matter of simply putting lipstick on a pig. The reframing we created helped people square off against the ugly reality they faced rather than ignore it.

Under this framework, the fear didn't disappear—it never will—but everyone was able to face it with greater resilience, one that comes from a deeper sense of meaning in the face of life's challenges. This resilience taps into a place within us where we recognize that no matter how difficult the circumstance, we have the capacity and the capability to respond from a place of reflection and learning.

The workers and managers were able to channel the energy the fear produced into productivity instead of paralysis. The workers who got laid off weren't unnecessary, unfortunate, or failures. They were heroes—people who made a sacrifice for the continued good of the factory and the town they all loved. The result was the most successful, and human-focused, plant shutdown in the organization's history.

With a sense of a higher purpose driving their work, the workers who knew they would be let go hit their production goals. On their last day of work, when the closing whistle blew, people hugged one another on the floor of the factory. As they left the factory for the last time, they walked past all the remaining employees, who applauded and saluted as their former coworkers marched off into the purple southern dusk.

As of 2019, the factory was back in growth mode and had rehired 20 to 30 percent of the laid-off employees.

Leadership in the Unfear Organization

A true unfear transformation changes almost everything about an organization, including its understanding of leadership, namely who the leaders are and how they should lead.

Who the Leaders Are

One of the core underpinnings of a fear-based organization is looking at leadership as a hierarchical concept, to see leadership as a role rather than as a state of mind. When leadership is seen as a role, it becomes about power, control, and aspiring to ever-increasing authority that ultimately leads to a corner office. In the unfear organization, leadership is a state of mind that all individuals have, irrespective of their roles. From this perspective, every individual is responsible for their mindset and growth, but leadership in unfear organizations is also a co-creative and communal activity that maximizes and multiplies the individual potential of its participants. This is partly why the effort at John's plant was so successful. Everyone in the organization stepped into their roles as leaders. They worked to develop new narratives around the layoffs and helped each other through their unfear transformations.

This does not mean that there is no hierarchy in an unfear organization. It just serves a different purpose. In a fear-based organization, hierarchy exists to put controls and limits on employees. In an unfear organization, hierarchy exists to streamline decision-making and remove impediments to learning so that all members of the organization can contribute to their fullest potential.

The Art of Drinking Poison Without Getting Poisoned

There is nothing easy about leadership. A small part of leadership is about technical expertise, but a large part is about working with humans, including yourself—humans who, given our endless complexity, are impossible to "solve" or manage through mathematical equations, a spreadsheet, or even machine learning. Leadership, then, is a highly complex art. There is an Indian myth that, for us, epitomizes the role of leadership.

According to the myth, every being in the universe, including the demigods and the demons, worked together to churn the Ocean of Milk to produce the Elixir of Life, which would bestow vitality and prosperity on them all. As they churned the ocean, all kinds of positive things emerged, including gems and the Wish-Fulfilling Tree. But as they continued to churn, a deadly poison flowed from the ocean and started killing humans, demigods, and demons alike. Worried that the poison would eradicate all life, everyone went to Shiva, one of the three supreme deities, and asked for help. Shiva took all the poison into his mouth and held it in his throat. He did not swallow it, so he was not poisoned. Cleared of the poison, the universe of living things thrived. Holding the poison turned Shiva's throat blue (Neela), and he was henceforth called Neelkantha.

The demigods and demons coming together to churn the Ocean of Milk is no different than when different parts of an organization come together to create something new. As the organization churns, it produces positive results, but also unintended new problems and challenges that spark fear and hinder the organization—this is the poison. The role of a leader (which is to say the role of everyone) is to take and hold that poison in their throats and help everyone else develop this ability. They can do this by reframing their relationship with fear. Instead of viewing fear as something that causes pain or that causes them to collapse into helplessness, they approach fear from a place of power. They recognize that they have the ability to rise above fear and to see it as an opportunity for learning—that they can choose their response: find energy and move forward in a productive way. They face the unintended outcomes and reframe the conversation around them to build resilience within the organization to deal with them in innovative ways.

This is what John eventually managed to do. He developed an environment in which everyone could be creative in the face of difficult circumstances and uncertainty. He created a space where people were not coddled or protected but were invited, as adults, to embrace the challenges of business as a learning opportunity.

> *In a fear-based organization, hierarchy exists to put controls and limits on employees. In an unfear organization, hierarchy exists to streamline decision-making and remove impediments to learning and create an environment where people are not coddled or protected but invited, as adults, to be creative contributors in the face of difficult circumstances and uncertainty.*

When an organization is able to reframe its relationship with fear, then fear and learning are no longer in contradiction. The organization develops the adaptability to face today's challenges as well as the unseen challenges of tomorrow.

That is the essence of unfear.

WORTH THINKING ABOUT

- What is your current story about the role or importance of fear at work?

- How or when do you find yourself caught in the dilemma of fear?

  ° Do you try to use fear to motivate others? Or yourself?

  ° Do you avoid fear or try to protect others from it?

- How are you or others in your organization responding to situations that generate fear today? How effective are those actions?

2

Biology of Fear and Unfear

O n a calm, beautiful late summer night in Annapolis, Maryland, I (Mark) carefully parallel parked my Toyota Tacoma on a one-way street. Originally designed for horse traffic in the 1600s, the streets of historic downtown Annapolis are charming but narrow. I checked my side view mirror to make sure that the coast was clear. I stepped onto the street, shutting and locking the door behind me.

Just then, bright headlights and a revving engine flooded my senses. A burst of energy shot through me, and I dived headfirst into the bed of my truck, anticipating an impact. SMASH! Something crashed against my lower leg, glass shattered, and metal crunched.

A vehicle roared past. Moments later, a police car followed, lights and sirens blaring.

In the bed of my truck, I checked to make sure I was in one piece. I was acutely aware of my surroundings, the feel of the plastic bed liner of the truck, the pattern of light and shadow from the streetlamp, the brick sidewalk. But I wasn't quite in tune with my body. I couldn't feel the lower part of my right leg, and I expected to see it hanging by a thread from the knee. Slowly, in a weirdly calm, almost trancelike state, I patted every part of my body—chest, thighs, knees, shins, feet. I'm all there. Nothing dangling, nothing missing. While I collected myself, a dazed bystander shuffled over in astonishment, "Oh my God, are you alright?"

"Yeah," I responded. And I was. I had just had a near-death experience, but already my heightened senses were slowly reverting to normal. My body was calming back down. Danger averted. I was safe.

I was lucky that the vehicle bearing down on me was an old-style pickup truck with folding side mirrors. The smashing glass and metal were just the mirror swinging back into the truck after hitting my leg. But that bit of luck would not have mattered at all if I hadn't dived out of the way. If I hadn't responded as quickly as I did, the drunk driver hurtling more than 60 miles per hour would have flattened me right there on the road. I only made that leap because I sensed a threat and felt an overwhelming degree of fear.

This story highlights why it's not only impossible, but also actually counterproductive to try to eradicate fear from an organization: *fear is essential to our survival.* Over the course of millions of years, we evolved the ability to feel fear and react to it by fighting the threat, fleeing from the threat, or freezing. However, we feel fear in countless situations that pose no direct threat to our survival. When we are not conscious of these behavioral patterns, our fear controls us and our reactions, often in such a subtle way that we are not even aware that we have given up control.

Yet, within all of us is the biological hardwiring to be an unfear individual. We can do this by recognizing these evolutionary patterns and not letting them cloud our judgment. By slowing down our emotional reactions and truly processing a situation before we respond, we can regain the ability to control our relationship with and the meaning that we make from fear.

Biology of Fear

In order to live as an unfear individual, you need to understand the evolutionary function of fear and how it can cause dysfunction in the modern world. Once you've done that, you'll instantly notice moments in everyday life when your evolutionarily programmed response to fear reduces your effectiveness—and begin to shift out of those patterns.

The Amygdala Hijack

According to neurobiologists, the threat-response circuit in our brain centers around the amygdala, an organ comprised of two almond-shaped glands that operates as an alarm system.[1] It constantly assesses sensory data—what you see, hear, and feel—for potential threats. Under normal, nonthreatening situations, your amygdala stays quiet and lets the rest of your brain function normally. When your amygdala senses a threat, it takes charge. It overrides the thinking, rationalizing, and planning parts of your brain (namely the prefrontal cortex) and launches you into immediate survival-oriented action. To give your body the fuel you need to stay alert and respond quickly to new threats, it also triggers the release of several hormones, including epinephrine (aka adrenaline), norepinephrine, and cortisol. Blood glucose spikes, and blood rushes to your limbs to enable you to move quickly.

That night in Annapolis, this process, wherein my entire body chemistry changed in less than a second, saved me from that hurtling truck. My amygdala interpreted the roar of the engine as dangerous and activated my survival system. Adrenaline shot into my bloodstream. My heart rate spiked; I jumped without thinking. Which is good, because I couldn't afford to stop and analyze the situation. I didn't have time to ask, "What's going on here? What kind of vehicle is that? How fast is this guy going? Should I run across the road? Why would someone be driving so fast here?" If I had tried to form even one of those questions in my mind, I wouldn't be here to tell the story. I responded before my "normal" thinking self could interrupt. Only in retrospect could I apply language to what had happened. The evolutionary advantage of this system is obvious, but it only works if the threat-response system can properly *identify* threats, which it rarely does.

The amygdala frequently activates in the face of no "real" threat because it sacrifices precision for speed. For example, I (Gaurav) have always been terrified of snakes. Once I took my 10-year-old daughter on a hike on Bear Mountain. It had rained the previous evening, so I was on the lookout for any snakes that might have washed out in the storm. Five minutes into our hike, I saw a snake out of the corner of my eye, and I yanked my daughter away. Once we both calmed down, we realized that the "snake" was actually a length of dirty rope.

The quick-trigger nature of the amygdala serves an evolutionary purpose: you can jump away from an old rope 1,000 times and still survive, but confuse a snake for an old piece of rope just once and you could die. Fortunately, in modern times, most of us rarely face life-threatening situations. Instead, we usually encounter emotional threats—for example, someone raising their voice when speaking, the pressure of a deadline, a friend not honoring their commitment, people invading our space, gossip, politics. The amygdala hasn't adapted to our newfound physical safety and remains hyperactive. Now it responds to these emotional threats. The response is exactly the same: we fight, we run (i.e., flight), or we freeze. Physiologically, the process is identical: adrenaline, cortisol, and glucose rush to the blood, and our heart rate increases. But there's nothing to physically do with all that excess energy. We can't dive into the bed of a truck to avoid criticism or physically lash out at someone who missed a deadline. Instead, we use that energy to stew on the perceived emotional threat, or we channel it in an unproductive way and lash out at whomever we think wronged us. Daniel Goleman, the internationally acclaimed psychologist and science journalist, calls this sort of immediate, disproportionate emotional response an *amygdala hijack*.

This is the fatal flaw in our hardwiring—the same process that ensures our physical survival lies at the root of so much human suffering and leads to dysfunctional social behaviors and outcomes, particularly in business. To manage this instinct, you need to understand what, exactly, our amygdala is trying to protect when it hijacks our system. An amygdala hijack only occurs when you perceive a threat to what psychologists refer to as the ego. Our ego is the carefully crafted image we portray to ourselves and to the world—it is our sense of self or identity. These beliefs—for example, "I'm a good person" or "I'm hardworking and talented"—are precious to us. They form the basis for how we imagine we should interact with the world and how the world should interact with us. We feel safe and comfortable when our beliefs about who we are go unchallenged. As soon as something happens to challenge this idea, the amygdala jumps into action.

Everyday situations at work often trigger amygdala hijacks. Depending on the context of the situation and your individual patterns, the hijack could manifest anywhere in the spectrum of fight, flight, or freeze reactions. For example, your boss asking, "Why hasn't your team met its quarterly goal?" could trigger a fear of failure, rejection, firing, and loss of livelihood. This could then turn into a fight reaction, so you say, "It's not my team's fault. The engineering team is holding everything up. They're the problem!" Or someone on your team makes a suggestion, "I think we should really be doing things this other way." This may activate your fear of being disrespected and rejected and result in a freeze reaction—a blank stare and awkward silence—while you scramble and fail to find something smart to say.

In our work, we see fight/flight/freeze responses lead to enormous daily waste. In more extreme cases, they can significantly impact entire careers. This happened to Miriam, whom we met when she was a nurse at a healthcare company where we led a transformation effort. She became inspired to do culture work of her own and scaled the corporate ladder, eventually becoming the head of culture and development. She was charming, excellent at motivating people, exceptionally talented in her field, and immensely popular and respected in the wider organization. Yet throughout her entire meteoric rise she suspected that senior management didn't respect her. Whenever management did something that confirmed this suspicion, she'd experience an amygdala hijack and question their commitment to sustaining the culture transformation that she and her team had accomplished.

Then the CEO, who was having his own fear-based reactions to a business challenge, reneged on a promise to make a substantial investment in Miriam's initiatives, removed some of her workshops from the budget, and reshuffled the organization so that Miriam reported to the head of human resources instead of directly to the CEO. Miriam perceived this as a personal attack against her and her work. She felt like her mentor had betrayed her by not protecting her. Overnight, she resigned from the organization that she had nurtured (and that had nurtured her) for over 10 years.

Several of the other leaders, who held deep respect for Miriam and considered her critical to the organization, asked her to return. But she felt so disrespected that their entreaties fell on deaf ears. It took almost six months before she realized that she could have made other choices. She might have found a way to resolve the issue and stay with the company. She might have decided it was impossible and come up with an exit strategy that allowed her to leverage the immense amount of goodwill she had built up to land her next assignment. She would have left carrying all the love and appreciation from her team and customers. Miriam's threat-response system stymied her own effectiveness. This isn't to say that the CEO didn't do anything ineffectual—he did. But Miriam's unexamined immediate response made her situation far worse.

In this story, both Miriam and the CEO held tightly to deep-seated fears and narratives around those fears. Additionally, they both operated in a fearful context. If they had recognized these circumstances and shifted them, then they could have potentially engaged in fruitful conversations and come to actions that better advanced their goals and those of the organization.

The bulk of this book covers how to reframe your, your team's, and your organization's relationship with fear so that it doesn't lead to such impulsive decisions and ineffectiveness. For now, however, you can take a step toward unfear by learning how to slow down and shorten an amygdala hijack. Don't ruminate on the issue. Let the adrenaline and glucose flow through and out of your veins, slow down your thoughts and reactions, and make sure that you've returned to a more reflective state before making a decision. This takes effort and practice, but it gets easier the more you do it and will help you tremendously on your unfear journey.

> *Take a step toward unfear by shortening an amygdala hijack. Don't ruminate on the issue. Let the adrenaline and glucose flow through and out of your veins, slow down your thoughts and reactions, and make sure that you've returned to a more reflective state before you make a decision.*

Negativity Bias: How We Know What to Fear

Miriam got caught in a downward spiral of interpretation and reaction. She believed that management didn't respect her, she saw examples of it, and this triggered her fight response. Management answered with fight responses of its own until the situation became unsustainable. This happens because of a psychological process called *negativity bias*. The process goes like this: in every moment, our brains notice and remember which conditions/stimuli feel safe/enjoyable and, more saliently, which feel threatening/dangerous/unenjoyable. Because we only have a finite amount of mental energy, we have to choose what to remember. Generally, remembering what is dangerous or threatening provides a greater survival advantage than remembering positive experiences (the two exceptions to this are the two positive experiences most important to our survival: eating and sex). For this reason, our brains tend to treat negative experiences like Velcro and cling to them. In contrast, our brains treat positive experiences like Teflon, and our memories of those experiences don't stick as firmly in our minds, no matter how vibrant or great the experience. Think about it, which of these memories from a young child matters more to survival: touching a hot burner to discover it hurts or a pleasant afternoon at the jungle gym with a best friend? This is one of the most fundamental processes that govern how we learn to navigate the world. We sort our experiences into pain and pleasure and attempt to avoid the former while moving toward the latter.

This process serves an evolutionary purpose—it helps us develop a large lifesaving index of threatening stimuli. When we encounter one of those stimuli in the world, it triggers the threat-response circuit. In Mark's story, his amygdala jumped into action because he already knew to associate a revving engine and approaching lights with a potential threat to his well-being. In contrast, in an organizational context, negativity bias can create dysfunction. Because of negativity bias, we are more likely to:

- Recall insults better than praise
- React more strongly to negative stimuli
- Remember traumatic experiences better than positive ones
- Dwell on unpleasant events more frequently than happy occurrences
- Make decisions in ways that minimize loss rather than generate optimal outcomes

In Miriam's story, her negativity bias reinforced her belief that her peers and colleagues didn't respect her. She likely believed that everyone saw her as "just" a nurse and not as someone who deserved to be the head of culture and transformation. She clung to every slight, real or perceived, and used it as evidence that she was undervalued. When the CEO cut her projects, she jumped right into the threat-response circuit because (1) the CEO's action confirmed what she had always expected and (2) she had strengthened her threat-response circuit by activating it so frequently in the past.

When we do not recognize how negativity bias shapes our perceptions, we are more likely to feel like we are at the mercy of our fears.

Over time, we learn to view more and more people and things in our environment as threats and become increasingly convinced that we have been wronged and that we must defend ourselves. However, when we recognize this tendency toward negativity, we can better assess situations and consciously work to remember positive experiences and moments of praise, kindness, and empathy from colleagues. We can learn to see people as humans and not as impediments or threats, and we can identify when an event throws us into an unnecessary amygdala hijack and make sure that we step out.

At an organizational level, negativity bias keeps us focused on all the threats in the environment and what can go wrong. While this helps with risk mitigation, it also can be demoralizing and prevent people from collaborating more effectively to solve problems. We start to see all the things that can go wrong but become blind to whether we're even solving the right problems in the first place.

Fear as a Habit

Have you ever driven your car to a familiar destination, parked, and suddenly realized that you have no idea how you got where you are? You know that you drove, but your mind was on such complete autopilot that you can't recall any details of the trip. Driving that specific route has become such an ingrained habit that it happened automatically. This is just one of several habits that dictate vast parts of our daily behavior: how we put our clothes on in the morning, how and when we brush our teeth, how often we check our phones throughout the day, what apps we use, how we use them, and so on. Habits simplify our lives. It takes less energy and focus to do something we've done before than to relearn how to do something every day.

Just as we form habits from our physical actions, we can also form them from our emotional responses. One of the most disruptive and pervasive habits is a reliance on fight, flight, and freeze responses. In other words, we can become addicted to the feeling of an amygdala hijack and constantly look for new negative stimuli to throw us into that hyperalert, reactive state. Do this enough, and fear becomes a mood, an orientation that we show up with every day, along with all the wasteful side effects it brings.

> *Just as we form habits from our physical actions, we can also form them from our emotional responses.*

To understand how this happens, we have to start with the science of habits. In his book *Atomic Habits*[2] entrepreneur James Clear proposes that habits form through four simple steps: cue, craving, response, and reward. To take a very basic example, we step into the kitchen and see a box of cookies (the cue). It makes us want a cookie because our brain wants a jolt of dopamine (craving). We eat the cookie (response), and we receive a jolt of dopamine (reward).

Over time, the associations between cue, craving, response, and reward become more and more hardwired in the circuitry of our brains. Hardwiring is more than a metaphor—our brains physically change as we develop habits. As we think and act in the world, our brains create connections among neurons. Whenever we repeat a thought or an action related to those connections, the connections grow stronger. The more we use them, the stronger they get; the less we use them, the weaker they get. As our brains physically change, our habits and automatic patterns change as well. Think about it like this: if you go for a walk every day in a meadow and follow the same general route, then over time you trample the grass sufficiently to create a clear path in the meadow. This makes it easier to follow that same path each day. The older path that you stopped using, while it never completely goes away, fades and recedes as grass begins to grow over it.

According to Clear, our prehistoric ancestors were paying attention to cues that signaled the location of primary rewards such as food, water, and sex. Today we spend most of our time learning cues that predict secondary rewards like money and fame, power and status, praise and approval, love and friendship, or a sense of personal satisfaction.

With few exceptions, most of the secondary rewards that Clear references are intimately connected to our egos. You might think of yourself as talented and intelligent and want your external reality to reinforce that self-image. That's the craving, which then leads you to follow a set of behaviors that you have associated with a reward or a satisfying fulfillment of the craving.

This is how we can fall into the habit of a fight/flight/freeze response—believing that those responses move us closer to attaining money, fame, status, and so on. For example, let's say that someone at work always shoots down your ideas in big meetings, before even listening to them. You consider yourself a creative problem solver, but this person clearly doesn't, and they make you look bad in front of everyone else. You interpret their dismissal as a threat to your ego. In the moment, this might even feel like a real threat to your physical well-being—the behavior of your coworker could cost you a promotion or even your job!

You're feeling a lack of control. Maybe this feels like that time you dealt with a bully in high school. Back then, you put the bully in their place, and after that, they left you alone. In the present day, you use the same tactic and exclaim, "Will you just please let me finish my point here?!" The outburst feels amazing. The person cutting you off retreats, and you can finish your argument. Sense of control reasserted, and maybe a couple of coworkers drop by your office after the meeting to thank you for finally standing up to that person.

This hypothetical situation goes through the four steps of habit building: the cue (big meeting, person stepping on your toes), the craving (fear of losing control and the desire to feel respected), the response ("Will you just let me finish . . . !"), and the reward (recapture the feeling of control and respect). Because your behavior worked to satisfy what you craved, you're more likely to engage in that kind of behavior again. If this happens often over a long enough period of time, fear-based knee-jerk responses become so pervasive that fear stops being a short-lived emotion to spark action and becomes a deeper, entrenched mood that dramatically reduces your overall effectiveness.

The truth is that all of us are, in some ways, addicted to the adrenaline hit that comes from an amygdala hijack. It gives us a sense of control, a sense that we are moving forward, taking action, and getting stuff done. Cable news and social media organizations know this, and they use it to capture interest. Have you ever wondered why there's a breaking-news banner every 40 seconds on CNN? Why you or others can't seem to stop scrolling through hundreds of pages of negative headlines on Facebook and Twitter? It's because we become addicted to finding and reacting to problems, even when they aren't there or aren't relevant to our daily lives. In organizations, this can manifest in what we a call a *firefighting culture*, in which everyone runs around in search of a crisis to resolve. The problem with firefighting cultures is that they create a lot of arsonists, people who light fires so that they have something to put out, to feed their own adrenaline addiction.

> *The more you are aware of and interrupt your habitual responses to fear, the weaker the neurologic pathways will become, and the less time you'll spend in a mood of fear.*

Being aware of how this process works can help you break your habitual reactions to fear. The next time you feel an urge to lash out at someone or to avoid a conversation, pause and reflect. What events led up to this feeling? Is there a pattern at play here? What other choices do you have in this moment? Where in your body do you feel this fear? The more you're aware of and interrupt this habit-forming process, the weaker the neurologic pathways will become, and the less time you'll spend in a mood of fear.

Fear Is Contagious

Once fear becomes a mood or a habit for one person in an organization, that mindset can quickly spread. This is because humans, as deeply social beings, mirror the emotions and behaviors of the people around them. As Dr. Sigal Barsade, an emotions researcher, explains, "We automatically mimic other people's facial expressions, body language, tone of voice—which we're hardwired to do from infancy. What happens next is also 'infectious': Through a variety of physiological and neurological processes, we actually feel the emotions we mimicked—and then act on them."[3]

In the hypothetical situation mentioned earlier, in which you push back against the person who keeps cutting you off, it is quite possible that your fear wasn't coming from you alone. It's possible that other people in the meeting were also feeling fear, which you contracted. Their body language and facial expressions subtly impacted your own body disposition. Maybe your heart started to beat a bit faster and some adrenaline was released into your system. Before the meeting even began, just being around these team members triggered some negative thoughts. And not only did others impact how you felt, your actions further reinforced and added to the fear already in the room. A snowball starts. . . .

This very human tendency explains why so many companies invest (and ultimately waste) nearly 20 percent of their time and effort managing people's egos.[4] One person with an unexamined relationship with fear, one negative comment, one perceived slight, can throw an entire office into a cascade of mutually reinforcing behaviors that waste time, energy, and talent.

The Costs of Fear

The costs associated with fear go beyond merely managing egos. Fear severely impacts individuals in organizations in two ways: health and well-being and performance.

Health and Well-Being

According to Wendy Suzuki, a neuroscientist and author of *Healthy Brain Happy Life*, high-stress work environments can create changes in our brain structure that are similar to those of post-traumatic stress disorder (PTSD), if not as acute or severe. In PTSD patients, the amygdala becomes larger and more overreactive, whereas the prefrontal cortex (the part of the brains responsible for emotional regulation and rational thought) shrinks.[5] Likewise, the hippocampus, which is implicated in making connections across the different parts of the brain in support of memory formation, imagination, and creativity, shrinks. In other words, the survival-threat circuit grows while the thinking part of the brain shrinks.

A high-stress work environment can literally change the structure of your brain and, in doing so, create massive negative impacts for the rest of your life.[6] These changes in the brain generate a constant state of hypervigilance, hyperreactivity, persistent stress, depression and anxiety, and impaired cognitive function. They also mean that many people walk around in a constant low-grade amygdala hijack, with all the hormones and extra glucose in their veins and the elevated pulse that comes with them. According to the American Psychological Association, this long-term elevation in heart rate, blood pressure, and stress hormones can increase the risk of hypertension, heart attack, or stroke. Additionally, other studies have shown that elevated stress levels damage our immune system by creating a state of chronic low-grade general inflammation that has been identified as "a possible prelude to various illnesses,"[7] including cardiovascular dysfunctions, diabetes, cancer, autoimmune syndromes, and mental illnesses such as depression and anxiety disorders.

Compounding the persistent stress in the workplace, a high percentage of employees show up with unresolved childhood trauma. According to the National Survey of Children's Health, almost half the children in the United States experience at least one or more types of adverse childhood experiences prior to entering adult life.[8] So many adults in the

United States are potentially walking around with persistent stress from various life experiences they had before even entering the workforce. Think about it: if nearly 50 percent of people already have hyperactive amygdalas, then throwing them into a high-pressure environment with little to no conversation about how to cope with and reframe their relationship with fear will only exacerbate existing psychological and physical health problems. So we invite you to have compassion for the life stories and experiences of every individual in the organization.

Fear Is Detrimental to Performance

From a performance perspective, fear and worry consume a great deal of energy. When we ruminate on our fears, we divert neural processing power away from more constructive tasks. This hinders our ability to dedicate sustained attention or deep thinking to a task.

Not only does individual performance suffer from chronic fear, but team and organizational performance does as well. In his book *Outliers*, Malcolm Gladwell examines why the majority of plane crashes happen while the pilot is flying the plane instead of the first officer. This would seem counterintuitive because pilots tend to have more experience and be more skilled at operating an aircraft. But flying requires collaboration between the two pilots, and effective collaboration requires effective, assertive communication. As Gladwell sums it up, "Planes are safer when the least experienced pilot is flying, because it means the second pilot isn't going to be afraid to speak up."[9]

The same process plays out in every organization and team. Because of the size and complexity of most organizations, though, it can be more difficult to identify how fear operates. This is because almost any outcome, positive or negative (e.g., plane crashes, business growth, a dip in profits), doesn't just come from one dramatic decision or change but from a long string of smaller actions and choices. In our experience, if you trace almost any negative outcome back far enough, you will find a dysfunctional relationship with fear as a significant contributing factor.

This holds true for something as simple as a missed deadline or handoff, when an employee, out of fear of being perceived as lazy or incapable, commits to something they can't actually do. It also holds true for systematic inefficiency that becomes ossified within an organization. For example, a leader might put several layers of approval in place for each project their team works on. Each of those layers probably came in response to a specific incident when somebody made a mistake or took some risky or ineffective action. The leader believes that they're just doing their job and that implementing all these wasteful layers is the only way to make sure that their team doesn't underperform. However, the leader based their beliefs on incomplete truths. The leader put the layers of approval in place because of their unexamined relationship with fear. There are other, more creative and potentially more effective ways to make sure employees don't make costly mistakes—such as coaching and training, communicating expectations earlier in a process, or even redesigning the process to make it simpler. But those ways take more time, and because they require the leader to sacrifice control and certainty, they often bump up against perceived threats. So, instead, the leader just decides it's easier to be the gatekeeper and slows down work for the entire team.

The Biology of Unfear: Language and Imagination

Humans are incredibly lucky. While almost every other animal experiences a version of the threat-response circuit, we are the only beings (we are aware of) that can *reflect* on these survival mechanisms, step back from a situation, interpret it, apply meaning to it, and choose the best path forward. We are the only ones who can change our relationship with fear so that it guides elevated performance instead of holding us in dysfunction. And we are able to do all this because we evolved two important superpowers: imagination and language.

These superpowers come from the newer parts of the human brain—specifically the prefrontal cortex (PFC). The PFC, which comprises most of the frontal lobes of the brain, is most strongly associated with executive function, personality, parts of speech and language, and the ability to modulate thoughts and emotions. With enough practice and skill, it can override the "lower-level" functions of the threat-response circuit. It is responsible for our capacity to imagine a future that doesn't exist yet, to set expectations, to create options and scenarios in our heads, and to plan. It is responsible for the mental representations we make of the world and of our place in it. This part of our brain gives us the unique capability to create and make novel choices.

Our closest living primate relatives, chimpanzees, share about 98.6 percent of our DNA, have structurally similar brains, and demonstrate many comparable behaviors that include expression of emotion, communication through touch and body language, and use of tools. Yet human brains are three times as big as those of chimpanzees, and specifically, our PFCs comprise a significantly higher percentage of our brains than those of chimpanzees.[10] These differences account for tremendous differences in cognitive capacity and variability in both individual and collective behavior.

While biology may drive our innate reactions to fearful stimuli, to unfear is to realize, clearly, that we are not constrained by this biology. For chimps and many other mammals, their biology is their destiny. Our superpowers enable humans to design our own future. Let's explore how this works for groups and individuals.

Language and imagination are intertwined. We imagine, and then, facilitated by language, we are able to make what we'd imagined, thought, and felt a reality. Language enables us to generate a future. For instance, if you ask someone on your team to meet with you on Thursday, at 2 p.m. and this person says yes, then you've both created a new future that didn't exist before. This happens so often in our lives that we rarely, if ever, stop to appreciate the magic that's taking place. Almost every achievement in human history comes from this combination of imagination and language. We can conjure new events, actions, structures, tools, and institutions.

Laws and money, for example, only exist and have value and meaning because of our collective imagining. At the same time, every human catastrophe—all the wars, injustices, and pain—come from these superpowers.

> *To unfear is to realize, clearly, that we are not constrained by our biology. Our superpowers enable humans to design our own future.*

Just as external language generates a collective future, our internal language generates our own future. This plays out in profound ways but also in simple, everyday situations. For example, let's say that your boss asks you for input on an important decision they need to make about a strategic initiative. *Internally*, you might say something like, "Here we go again. I'm being asked to support this horrible project that's doomed to fail. But my boss won't tolerate someone who's not a team player, and if I raise any concerns, they'll lash out against me." But externally, you tell your boss, "That sounds great!" Here your internal conversation already ensures that your concerns won't be addressed because you're convinced that any effort would prove futile, so you don't even try to improve the situation. Not only that, but chances are good that your body language will convey some disconnect between what you're saying externally versus internally. This can lead to a breakdown in trust and effective communication.

In this hypothetical situation, you are operating as if you are at the mercy of your fears, like you don't have a choice. Yet our superpowers give us choice in the face of that fear. We can either react to it, fall into an amygdala hijack and all the other biological patterns that we have described, or we can use our superpowers to realize that we are in control of our relationship with fear. We can behave like Elon Musk, who imagined the electric car as a way of revolutionizing the industry, or like traditional car manufacturers, who convinced themselves that it was just a fad.

This creates new possibilities and a new future for us. We can choose to reframe fear and stop viewing a particular situation as a threat and instead see it as an invitation to learn, as a sign that we are stepping outside of our comfort zones. Instead of viewing friction with a colleague as a threat to our career prospects or ego, we can look at it as an invitation to learn how to handle this situation in an effective way and grow from the experience. Instead of passively marching down our evolutionarily created neuropathways, we can use our adaptable brains to our advantage and make different, less reactive, and more effective choices.

Admittedly, at the start, this is incredibly difficult. It takes far less energy to follow the evolutionarily wired pathways in our brain. But we can train ourselves to do it, to look at emotional threats and ask, "How can I grow from this experience? What are the positive possibilities in this situation?" This is a step that requires a tremendous amount of courage, but it will set you on a path toward unfear.

> *It takes far less energy to passively follow the evolutionarily wired pathways in our brain. But we can train ourselves to look at emotional threats and ask, "How can I grow from this experience? What are the positive possibilities in this situation?"*

We must wield our superpowers wisely. Just as we can use our imagination and language to shift into unfear, we can use both to further reinforce dysfunctional, reactive narratives around fear and further strengthen and activate our threat-response circuits in situations that don't call for them. In Chapter 3 we explore these dysfunctional stories about fear in detail and examine the common behavioral patterns they produce. Then in Part II we discuss how to change those stories and start an unfear transformation in yourself, your team, and your organization.

WORTH THINKING ABOUT

- How do you experience fear in your workplace?

- What threats are you currently perceiving? Are they physical or emotional?

- Do you tend to fight, flee, or freeze when facing threats? How does this change with the context?

- How might the experience of fear be impacting your or others' performance and well-being?

3

Eight Fear Archetypes
in the Workplace

Think of the patterns of behaviors that you usually see in an organization: teamwork, coaching, initiative taking, innovation, bureaucracy, power plays, gossiping, scapegoating, backstabbing, and so on. The confluence of all the behaviors in an organization leads to high performance or to dysfunction—or, more often than not, some combination or interplay of the two.

What most people don't realize is that to an extent, all these behaviors are external manifestations of how we relate to fear. When we aren't aware of this, we remain stuck in biologically hardwired reactions. Organizations and the people within them blindly live at the mercy of their fears, and when they do, they are more likely to display dysfunctional behaviors. To describe this phenomenon, we have identified eight broad patterns of reactive behavior that we call *fear archetypes*. These archetypes were created by synthesizing our experiences of working with organizations with the work of researchers and organizational culture experts Robert Cooke, J. Clayton Lafferty, and Janet Szumal,[1] and the diagnostic tools developed by their organization, Human Synergistics International. These archetypes fall into two groups depending on whether the fear response is fight based or flight/freeze based. Following the work of Cooke, Lafferty, and Szumal, we call fight-based responses *Aggressive/Defensive* and flight/freeze-based responses *Passive/Defensive* (Figure 3.1).

> The Fear Archetypes are derived from the Organization Culture Inventory® (OCI®) developed by Human Synergistics International in the 1980s. The OCI is recognized as one of the most widely used and thoroughly researched organization culture tools in the world. Please refer to the Appendix for more details about the tool and how it is linked to the Fear Archetypes.

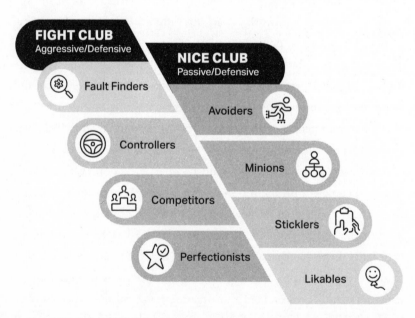

The distinction between Passive/Defensive and Aggressive/Defensive styles, as well as the names of some of the archetypes, are from the *Organizational Culture Inventory*® by Robert A. Cooke and J. Clayton Lafferty (1987). Copyright © Human Synergistics International. All Rights Reserved. Used by Permission.

FIGURE 3.1   Fear archetypes

All these archetypes are based on good intentions and values and can, at times, produce positive results. However, any strength overplayed can become a weakness. And this is what these archetypes describe: people who rely on their strengths so obsessively or mindlessly that their behavior becomes dysfunctional.

> *Any strength overplayed can become a weakness.*

As you go through this chapter, we invite you to reflect on which of these archetypes you, your team, and your organization tend to slip into and in what situations. We all have some tendency to display one or a combination of these styles, especially under stress.

If you see yourself in any of these styles, we are not saying that's who you are and who you will always be. What we are saying is that these are often unconscious patterns that arise from how you habitually react to fear. You may have a go-to pattern, but you're not fixed in that pattern. The same holds true if you see your colleagues in a specific archetype. You can change; so can they. So let's not judge ourselves or other people for falling into these patterns. So many of the dysfunctional behaviors we describe come from a place of good intentions, from a desire to help the organization succeed, produce high-quality work, maintain safety, and so on. But while the intentions may be good, they often create several unintended negative outcomes.

Keep in mind that any such classification is, by definition, an oversimplification of complex dynamics. We can identify and parse out each archetype, yet the reality is that people and groups demonstrate a wonderful mix and intensity level of these various styles. This happens because the way each individual responds to fear depends on several factors, including, to name a few, genetic predispositions, life experiences (particularly those in the formative childhood years), cultural context, upbringing, learning over the years, and, of course, the environmental context of the action.

That said, these archetypes help us notice patterns of behavior, and this awareness alone can be transformative. We can leverage our superpowers to realize that we don't have to be stuck in these archetypes.

The Fight Club: Aggressive/Defensive Archetypes

These sorts of behaviors might be summed up as "the best defense is a strong offense." People who display these behaviors often go on the attack in order to feel safe. *Aggressive/Defensive* patterns are built by putting what is best for the self or one's own tribe over the long-term interest of the entire organization and its stakeholders. In the world of emotional fear, this category of behaviors describes the active, confrontational measures people take to protect their status and security. This group is motivated by a desire to prove to the world their "specialness" (in terms of talent, intelligence, accomplishments, work ethic, etc.) as a protective response to threats. People or groups with these tendencies put down or scapegoat others to avoid showing vulnerability or admitting mistakes, which impedes their own ability to reflect and grow. For each of the archetypes, we identify the dysfunctional stories they tell themselves, their positive values and intentions, and their negative outcomes.

> *We can leverage our superpowers to realize that we don't have to be stuck in these archetypes.*

 Fault Finders

Fault Finders[2] believe that personal and organizational power comes from identifying and preventing problems. Fault Finders think that highlighting all the things that aren't right with themselves, others, and circumstances will prevent unhappy surprises and demonstrate to the world their competence and worth. To keep themselves safe, they identify all the faults and deficiencies they can find in their environment or in the people with whom they interact.

Fault Finders value their contributions to collective efforts. They value problem identification and solving. They desire continuous improvement and environments in which people have high standards for themselves and others. Because of this, they have a discerning eye and can point out where things could have been done differently or better. They also can detect and mitigate risks associated with a given action that other people miss.

However, their dysfunctional relationship with fear causes Fault Finders to weaponize their discerning eye. This leads to excessive judgment of ideas and other people. A Fault-Finding culture tends to get caught up in unnecessary conflict that leads to stagnation because everyone spends more time identifying problems than solving them. When companies with a Fault-Finding culture do solve problems, they settle on the solutions that have the least "faults," which tend to be safe but are often ineffective or narrow in scope.

A Fault-Finding culture looks a lot like this: You walk into an important strategy meeting to propose a direction for the department to members of the executive team. Just as you're about to present, one of the executives asks, "Why haven't you invited the head of procurement to this meeting?"

It all goes downhill from there. As you present the vision, people poke holes in the logic or ask for implementation details that you don't have on the slides. When you ask the group for ideas, they offer all the reasons why your suggestions will never work. Perhaps most frustrating of all, someone perks up and says that on page 5, line 6, the font size is 10 points when the company standard is 12. We are, of course, exaggerating a little for effect, but you get the picture. Fault Finders defend themselves and their egos by attacking others, opposing new ideas, being critical of others and their work, and making safe decisions to avoid criticism.

Fault Finders* Archetype Profile

Leaders	• Exert superiority by finding fault in employees' work • Make employees feel defensive rather than supported; give extensive critical feedback rather than supportive coaching • Demonstrate little flexibility in their points of view and refuse to accept criticism or feedback from subordinates • Remain aloof from the team and situation
Employees	• Focus on pointing out mistakes of colleagues; focus on what is going wrong much more than what is going well • Gossip about people and their weaknesses • Oppose or point out the downsides of new initiatives and ideas • Do not ask for help out of fear of being criticized or seen as underperformers
Teams	• Focus on pointing out the mistakes of other groups and shifting blame • Create barriers and challenges to creative thinking or exploration of new, untested solutions
Organization	• Rewards its members for being critical of others and opposing new ideas • Is critical and judgmental of those outside the organization (e.g., customers, competitors, etc.) • Fosters confrontation and constant scrutiny

*The descriptors of Fault Finders are based on our experience with organizations and include items from the *Organizational Culture Inventory®* by Robert A. Cooke and J. Clayton Lafferty (1987). Copyright © Human Synergistics International. All Rights Reserved. Used by Permission.

 ## Controllers

We all have a little bit of the *Controller*[3] in us—it's that desire to be able to predict the outcome of our choices, to be certain about our future, to keep the unruly forces of chaos at bay. Controllers tend to believe that the world is a dangerous place and that their power or that of the group comes solely from their ability to control outcomes. And positive outcomes are synonymous with self-worth.

Controllers value stability and respect. They sense that uncertainty, if not managed or understood properly, can lead to bad outcomes. They see and respond to risks and uncertainty in the environment. Rather than leave roles and responsibilities ambiguous, for instance, they create clear lanes for action and decision-making.

The instinct to exercise control is the primary driving force behind most of the social, governmental, and technological innovations in human history. From fire, to tools, to agriculture, to laws, to governments, to cars, to corporations, to computers, humans have sought to exert control over the uncertain forces of nature and other people. Control is useful. It provides stability, helps us attain what we desire, and helps us survive.

Controllers protect themselves by micromanaging subordinates, keeping decision-making power to themselves, and leveraging their expertise to dictate each point of a solution. Often Controllers will prioritize the hierarchy of an organization and yield power to their superiors while keeping a tight rein over their subordinates. In our experience, controlling behaviors emerge most often in senior levels of organizations or in situations where expertise is critical to decision-making (e.g., the lead doctor on a traditional surgical team). In many situations, this need to control comes from a lack of confidence. The Controller attempts to manipulate the external world in order to control and manage their fear of their internal world.

This has a predictable effect: a controlling culture disempowers most members in an organization and empowers those at the top. An employee's worth is determined by his or her location in the hierarchy, not by the employee's actual contributions. This leads employees to hold back their ideas and knowledge and become dependent on leaders for direction and decisions. It's safer not to upset the existing structures and egos of those in charge. The overt discipline and structure seen in these kinds of organizations create (and often hide) the resentment that employees feel.

One of the most quintessential Controllers we have ever met once blurted out, "This is not a democracy!" He was a senior political appointee in a federal government agency who hired us to improve the effectiveness and decision-making in his department. Even though the members of his team had great prior corporate work experience and were highly capable, they showed up with a negative attitude and only did what they

 Controllers* Archetype Profile

Leaders	• Use position in the hierarchy to control subordinates and their actions
	• Never relinquish control and maintain unquestioned authority
	• Demand loyalty
	• Build fiefdoms
	• Attempt to be on top of everything
Employees	• Do not share information or knowledge in order to control others
	• Use expertise as a tool of control and status rather than a source of shared knowledge
	• Tend to be on the attack in interactions
	• Engage in politics to maintain and enhance status
Teams	• Act forcefully in their interactions with other teams
	• Withhold information from other groups to establish their superiority
	• Engage in politics to maintain status relative to other teams or groups
Organization	• Encourages hierarchical thinking and decision-making among members
	• Improvement ideas only come from the top or established experts
	• Emphasizes formal chain of command and discipline over entrepreneurship and empowerment
	• Dictates terms and outcomes to customers and other stakeholders

* The descriptors of Controllers are based on our experience with organizations and include items from the *Organizational Culture Inventory®* —copyrighted © by, and with the permission of, Human Synergistics International.

were told. Despite impressive backgrounds and accomplishments, they didn't show any initiative. When we spoke with the appointee's team, we discovered that none of them were allowed to make their own decisions. They often had to wait weeks for the leader's approval, and in situations of disagreement, the leader's point of view always prevailed.

After our discussions with employees, we suggested to the leader that his behavior stymied his employees. This was when he very clearly announced that this wasn't a democracy and that he didn't hire us to fix him, but his employees. Ironically, this leader wanted his team to take more initiative. Even after our discussions, the leader wouldn't budge. Not surprisingly, the team struggled to create any meaningful cultural shift toward their stated goals of "initiative" and "accountability."

Competitors

Competitors[4] believe that their worth and value are synonymous with how they compare with others. They believe that the path to acceptance and love is through besting others and being recognized for it. Competitors seek security in life by winning. They perceive the world as being made up of winners and losers, and they're very clear about which camp they want to be in. This is a deeply individualistic orientation, primarily motivated by a desire to compare favorably with others. Competitors seek achievement to make themselves look better than others instead of seeking achievement to create a personal or collective sense of satisfaction.

Competitors value achievement, improvement, and recognition. These can be forces for good. Companies need to compete for customers and market share. This can drive important improvements in products, services, and internal operations over time. Companies compete for talented people, which often drives companies to offer better work environments over time. Within companies, the ideas offered by individual employees compete to determine the path forward on a key project. All these mini competitions can drive the performance of a business, but only if they don't spill over into dysfunction.

An excessively Competitive culture values winning above everything and actively encourages internal competitiveness. This results in reduced effectiveness, silos, and unrealistic standards of performance that lead to missed opportunities for collaboration, learning, and improvement. It also drains the joy out of work and creates burnout and exhaustion. For Competitors, good is never enough. They have to do better than others. The constant comparison with others leaves big blind spots, wastes energy, and shuts down learning. If left unchecked, a culture dedicated to winning tends to ignore the organization's core values. This can lead to counterproductive and unethical practices. The story of Enron's rise and fall, for instance, offers one cautionary tale about the downsides of excessive competition.

I (Mark) have identified quite strongly with this archetype through most of my adult life. I distinctly remember the day I was cut from the junior high school baseball team and the day I broke my finger and couldn't finish tryouts for the high school basketball team. These experiences were painful. I felt like a loser. I subscribed to the story that only winners would be popular, have fun in life, and be successful. Eventually, I poured my heart and soul into golf. I was very good at it. I started winning golf tournaments and won a golf scholarship to college.

While my dreams of playing on the PGA Tour were dashed fairly early in my college career, the competitive drive within me remained. Fueled by fear of being seen as a loser, I worked hard to win wherever I found myself. I pushed myself to get A's in college, be seen as a top achiever in my units in the Navy, start my nonmilitary career at one of the top consulting firms in the world, and strive to be better than my peers at McKinsey.

While this competitive orientation spurred me to work hard and achieve, it also came with a huge and largely unacknowledged dark side. I was extremely hard on myself. I became judgmental of myself and others. I lost the joy of playing golf and instead found only disappointment and anger. I was prickly and insecure at times in my early Navy days. I experienced burnout and exhaustion in my consulting work. I was on a never-ending treadmill of chasing short-term wins but rarely questioning the longer-term consequences of those efforts on my performance and well-being or on others. The Competitor within me was driven by fear, and for a long time, I just couldn't see that or how to get beyond it.

 ## Competitors* Archetype Profile

Leaders	• Focus on being right and not entertaining challenges from direct reports • Take credit for the team's effort and put themselves in the limelight • Will never appear to lose even if it means throwing someone from the team under the bus
Employees	• Try hard to be the center of attention and maintain an image of superiority • Want to outperform peers and team members and be recognized as the most indispensable person on the team • Compete instead of cooperate • Place significant emphasis on formal evaluations and rewards as a measure of self-worth
Teams	• Limit collaboration with other parts of the organization • Make your team look good at the expense of other teams • See team membership as more important than organizational membership
Organization	• Often highly fragmented with little or ineffective collaboration • Siloed thinking and processes; limited cross-functional or value stream collaboration • Limited best practice sharing across teams • Tend to create unrealistic standards of performance

*The descriptors of Competitors are based on our experience with organizations and include items from the *Organizational Culture Inventory®* —copyrighted © by, and with the permission of, Human Synergistics International.

Perfectionists

Perfectionists[5] believe that their worth and safety are synonymous with the quality of their output. Mistakes, errors, and problems indicate their insufficiency and unworthiness—so they work extra hard to prove to the world that they're worthy. Perfectionistic cultures believe that heroic human efforts achieve perfection. They discount systemic ways to improve quality and excellence while celebrating extrahuman efforts, no matter how much waste they produce.

Perfectionists value high-quality work and high standards of achievement. Many industries require this level of attention to detail: nuclear power, industrial chemicals, high-tech or precision manufacturing, the military, healthcare, and aviation. In most of these industries, sloppiness could result in death. Even in less dramatic situations, consistent quality can make the difference between a successful long-term strategy and one that fails. High-risk, high-uncertainty industries or roles (e.g., investing, underwriting, marketing, or product development) face difficult choices about when a product or decision is "ready." A desire to get things right in these situations is well founded and necessary.

Perfectionists make themselves feel safe by avoiding mistakes at all costs. They keep track of everything, dot all the i's and cross all the t's, and work long hours to attain narrowly defined goals. When a Perfectionist delivers something, it is a thing of beauty. However, the Perfectionist way of working also creates various problems. Perfectionists define *perfect* by their own standards instead of the standards of their customers. Because of this, they attempt to control each aspect of the process so that the product meets their exact vision. This silences other voices. Perfectionists often get so lost in the details that they fail to adjust to changing priorities. Often, when they finally look up to survey the broader situation, they discover that they've been trying to solve the wrong problem.

Perfectionists insist that any activity related to quality can't be questioned or changed. As a result, they miss all kinds of opportunities to avoid excess processing and rework. Members of Perfectionist cultures tend to show symptoms of strain and stress. They may have a story about how necessary their efforts are, but they're exhausted and drained at the same time.

Given the success of Apple over the last two decades, it is easy to forget just how tumultuous and tenuous its early years were under Steve Jobs. According to the biography by Walter Isaacson,[6] Jobs was a notorious Perfectionist. People found him difficult to work with, and his obsessive tinkering nearly sank some of the company's early and most important products. While Jobs was unquestionably visionary, he was also extremely lucky. The launch of the original Macintosh, for instance, was more than two years behind schedule but ended up being successful in part because some Competitors slipped up.

The conflict stemming from Jobs's perfectionism caused his departure from Apple shortly after the launch of the Macintosh. Isaacson suggests that during the 10 years Jobs spent away from the company, he learned to soften his leadership style and to allow more voices into the creative process. In short, he learned to let go of some of the hard-driving Perfectionist tendencies he'd clung to. He was much more successful the second time around, launching Apple on a strong trajectory with world-changing products such as the iPhone.

Overall, Perfectionists struggle with efficiency and balance. They spend most of their time toiling on the few final details of a task rather than getting feedback and input much earlier in the process. All of these dynamics create situations that make it difficult for individuals and groups to learn quickly and collaborate their way to achieving meaningful goals. Perfectionists struggle mightily to work in agile environments where small and potentially imperfect outputs are created and tested at frequent intervals.

Perfectionists* Archetype Profile

Leaders	• Obsessively check outputs of the team, leading to slow decision-making • Personally intervene in processes that others can handle • Set unrealistically high goals
Employees	• Excessively precise and lose focus on the bigger picture • Attempt to never make a mistake • Persist, endure, and ask for help too late in the process • Rarely work with ease and joy; feel burnt out
Teams	• Often lose connection with the broader organization and lose focus on the broader goals of the company • Oriented to short-term team targets to the exception of everything else
Organization	• Create unrealistically high and potentially irrelevant goals/standards • Spend significant time and energy creating "perfect" plans that never see the light of day • Create cumbersome approval and oversight processes • Become overly risk averse and slow to make decisions • Lose connection with customer needs and shifts in the market; become excessively internally focused

* The descriptors of Perfectionists are based on our experience with organizations and include items from the *Organizational Culture Inventory®* —copyrighted © by, and with the permission of, Human Synergistics International.

The Nice Club: Passive/Defensive Archetypes

People or organizations exhibiting these behaviors (flight or freeze responses) hide from impending threats. They focus on smoothing over what's uncomfortable and putting on a happy face. When things go wrong, they divert attention elsewhere or deflect responsibility. This prevents people from asking questions, sharing dissenting points of view with colleagues, and challenging existing practices directly.

Passive/Defensive culture norms are grounded in the management philosophy that the average employee dislikes work and will try to get away with doing the bare minimum. Passive/Defensive leaders believe the best way to motivate people is through tight controls or rules, clear direction, and punitive action if those rules or directions are not followed. Over time, this philosophy leads to workplaces where employees, in the quest for safety and job preservation, prefer to be directed and avoid taking responsibility and ownership. In a way, a strong Passive/Defensive culture is one in which most people have a degree of learned helplessness.

Organizations with a Passive/Defensive culture can survive for a while, but only in highly stable environments with minimal competition. They struggle tremendously when facing competition or the general uncertainty of the modern business environment.

 ## Avoiders

Avoiders[7] believe that conflict and chaos are dangerous. They believe that it is riskier to take action than it is to play it safe and do nothing. This archetype seeks safety by avoiding any conflicts or uncomfortable/uncertain situations. Avoiders doubt their ability to manage these situations and perceive the workplace as a minefield where any step they take might lead to an explosion.

Avoiders value peace and reflection. They avoid drama. Where Aggressive/Defensive people or teams can stir up unproductive conflict, Avoiders see the dysfunction in those dynamics and steer clear of it. They may not understand the dysfunction in their own behaviors (or nonbehaviors), but at least they don't actively add fuel to the fire.

An organization with an Avoider culture encourages inaction in the face of challenging situations in the exact moments when they need action. Members tend to look the other way, gloss over problems, and resist taking even the most calculated of risks. These organizations get stuck in their comfort zone and struggle to adapt to their environment. Avoider-oriented cultures lack energy, inspiration, and continuous improvement.

They may keep their heads down to meet the demands of today, but they're not creating the conditions to meet the demands of tomorrow. At best, they get by.

A common example of Avoiders in organizations are people or teams that avoid naming the uncomfortable issues or "elephants in the room."

 ## Avoiders* Archetype Profile

Leaders	• Make popular rather than necessary decisions
	• Often procrastinate/delay key decisions
	• Offer vague feedback
	• Take the back seat, leaving the driving to others
Employees	• Avoid making clear commitments, always leaving themselves wiggle room
	• Lie low when the going gets tough and wait for others to act first
	• Make sure others are blamed for problems, even when they made the mistake
	• Give excuses for why something cannot be done
Teams	• Become the bottleneck in the value chain
	• Wait to make decisions until the direction the rest of the company is moving in is known
	• Cement the siloes by pushing decisions upward and delaying action
	• Often change their stance on important issues to avoid conflict with others
Organization	• Oriented toward avoiding failure; specify and create consequences for failure but don't reward success
	• Move slowly/cautiously in response to external threats or changes in the competitive environment
	• Avoid challenging assumptions and continue past practices, stifling efforts at continuous improvement
	• Don't discuss mistakes and end up repeating them

*The descriptors of Avoiders are based on our experience with organizations and include items from the *Organizational Culture Inventory®* —copyrighted © by, and with the permission of, Human Synergistics International.

For instance, before the pandemic, we worked with one government agency where managers were convinced that some employees were abusing telework policies. At the same time, other employees had recently filed grievances through the union about unfair treatment by managers. The managers didn't want to address telework with the employees out of fear that they would spawn more grievances. The employees, meanwhile, didn't feel like they could safely discuss their needs without upsetting other employees or the union representatives. The union representatives were afraid that if they talked with the managers, they'd look weak. To everyone, the uneasy détente among these groups seemed better than taking any action. Needless to say, when this kind of fear is going on, no real conversations about telework happened and no creative solutions materialized. Everyone avoided the topic. No one was happy.

 ## Minions

Minions[8] believe that success is directly related to what the boss thinks of them. They draw their sense of worth from others with more expertise and positional power. For Minions, the only customer is the boss. Minions seek safety in current power structures, being good followers, keeping their heads down, and not rocking the boat. They live by the mantra, "Do what you're told, and we'll all be fine."

Minions value tradition, respect, and safety. They understand the value of clear roles and responsibilities and how hierarchical structures can help effectively regulate the flow of information and resources in organizations. They acknowledge the expertise and responsibilities of others and have no problem giving people with the proper expertise the power to make decisions.

A Minion-oriented culture, more than any other, shifts the focus away from pleasing customers toward serving the bosses. This creates an insular organization that wastes valuable energy and talent on internal power instead of value-added work. Minions tend to adopt a helpless or passive stance in the face of challenges. They look to others to provide guidance.

Companies with a strong Minion culture usually put far too much decision-making power at the top of the hierarchy. This has four effects. First, decision quality suffers because leaders receive minimal input from the employees who have a more accurate sense of the frontline reality. Second, top leaders or select experts drive improvement efforts without soliciting the ideas and talents of most people in the organization. Third, a Minion

 Minions* Archetype Profile

Leaders	• Act like parents toward the team, treating them like children (to be protected and/or directed) • Do not defend the team in front of senior management • Accept senior management's goals and expectations without question • Are patient and predictable in following upper management but mercurial and quick-tempered with their own teams
Employees	• Seek to please those in positions of authority • Constantly check decisions with superiors • Follow directives, even when they are wrong or misguided • Feel disconnected from the mission and purpose of the organization beyond pursuing the priorities of top leaders
Teams	• Are timid in the face of challenges • Focus on pleasing those in authority rather than their role in the value stream • Easily conflate task conflict and relationship conflict—and avoid both
Organization	• Are highly centralized, with hierarchical decision-making processes • Leadership and employees show minimal initiative • Avoid risk in the marketplace; follow trends rather than set them • Key leaders and experts drive improvement efforts while minimizing input and energy from most of the organization

*The descriptors of Minions are based on our experience with organizations and include items from the *Organizational Culture Inventory®* —copyrighted © by, and with the permission of, Human Synergistics International.

culture creates rigid and bureaucratic processes. A few people at the top need to sign off on everything, which reduces agility. Fourth, most of the talented and motivated people leave for organizations where they have more autonomy and freedom, leaving a higher percentage of Minions behind.

Minion cultures are almost always found in organizations with leaders who demonstrate strong Controller tendencies. In these organizations, employees frequently reference the leader as the reason why they're doing something or prioritizing a particular task. They also obsess over the leader's emotional state in interactions because it will have an outsized impact on their day.

In a technology company we worked with recently, most people in the organization pointed to the CEO as the reason they were working on something even if they didn't agree with it as opposed to framing their work in terms of how it contributed to the organization's or customers' outcomes. This CEO's moods were a main topic of conversation as well. If the CEO was in a good mood, so was everyone else. If she was in a distressed mood, employees took on that level of distress. They were all locked in a fear-based dance.

Sticklers

Sticklers[9] believe that obsessively following the rules will protect their sense of worth and power. Rules become a shield to be used for protection rather than a way to achieve positive outcomes for everyone. Sticklers view rules as a source of security and an unassailable statement of truth.

Sticklers value tradition, the wisdom of the past, and consistency. They cherish fairness and equity. Like hierarchies, rules have their place in high-performing organizations. In high-risk industries (e.g., aviation, nuclear power, healthcare), following rules and established precedent is absolutely essential for safe and reliable operations and effective decision-making. These kinds of rules were born out of years of trial and error.

A Stickler-focused culture, like a Minion culture, creates the expectation that members will follow others instead of taking initiative. The difference is that a Minion follows a certain person in the hierarchy, whereas a Stickler serves an abstract hierarchy. Sticklers rely on the rule book, the established best practices, and company norms to make them feel safe in the face of pushback or uncertainty. Sticklers are so risk adverse that even if the leader explicitly tells them to disregard the rules, they'll push back and say the rules are most important. They shun creative approaches as unreliable and view those who try new things with suspicion. Because of this, organizations with a Stickler culture struggle with continuous improvement. The rules become rigid and fixed as opposed to living, evolving stores of knowledge and wisdom about how to achieve desired results.

Whenever we start a new consulting project, we ask our clients, "Why do you do it this way?," referencing important practices in the work environment. Whenever we hear, "Because that's how it's supposed to be done," we know that the organization has a strong Stickler tendency. Individuals and groups with this pattern often succeed in introducing new ways of working (e.g., lean or agile practices) across large groups of people but struggle to create a true culture of experimentation or continuous improvement.

In 2017, a particularly visceral example of dysfunctional rule following went viral when United Airlines forcibly removed Dr. David Dao from an overbooked flight. United policy called for some passengers to be removed to make space for others in certain circumstances. The United employees were just following the rules that day as they dragged Dr. Dao screaming and bloodied out of his seat, down the aisle, and off the plane. The next day, the CEO sent an email to employees praising them for following the rules. It can be easy to demonize United Airlines for this and act like its employees were behaving in some evil way. This is potentially misguided. We take this incident as an indication that United has a powerful Stickler culture. Aviation has become one of the safest consumer industries in the world in spite of the fact that it is one of the riskiest. This is, in part, because of rule following. United requires extensive rules and bylaws to successfully fly and land hundreds of planes a day. In such an environment, it would make perfect sense for well-intentioned employees to follow the rules as closely as possible in a moment of uncertainty. As the company found out, sometimes this can be a mistake.

Sticklers* Archetype Profile

Leaders	• Kill new ideas or ideas that violate spoken/unspoken rules • Focus on enforcing rules and standardized procedures over all else, including common sense and creativity • Emphasize form over substance
Employees	• Conform and make a good impression • Follow the letter of the law, instead of the spirit of the law • Always accept the status quo; don't question how things have been done in the past • Emphasize rules as more important than ideas • Fit into expected "mold"
Teams	• Are inflexible to shifts in deliverables or timing • Do not deviate from standards to adapt to the situation
Organization	• Are bureaucratically controlled • Have conventional and highly centralized decision-making • Are rigid in the face of changing circumstances • Lack creative, out-of-the box thinking • Lack innovation and continuous improvement of products, services, and internal operations

*The descriptors of Sticklers are based on our experience with organizations and include items from the *Organizational Culture Inventory®* —copyrighted © by, and with the permission of, Human Synergistics International.

 ## Likables

Likables[10] believe that how other people feel about them determines their self-worth. Acceptance within a group is synonymous with safety and success. Likables believe that conflict is highly dangerous to trust and strong relationships.

Likables value trust, harmony, teamwork, and collaboration. Likables understand that trust and a sense of safety and belonging are essential to high performance. When they try to appease everybody, they do it because they believe that is how you build a high-performing team.

Likable individuals and groups obscure and gloss over the real issues they face. They play nice and go with the flow, even when pressing problems exist. Difficult conversations don't take place, creative tension never arises, and meaningful problem solving rarely occurs. The collective organization stays in its comfort zone, and performance slowly fades over time.

Likables tend to take what people say or do personally and confuse productive, task-focused conflict and disagreement with destructive, relationship-based conflict. In an attempt to make everyone happy, they minimize disagreements, which can lead to stagnation.

A team or organization comprised of several Likables often will fall prey to what management expert Jerry B. Harvey calls the *Abilene*

Likables* Archetype Profile

Leaders	• Seek to please everyone and build consensus • Delay final decisions • Struggle to communicate unpopular messages
Employees	• Try to stay on the good side of people and be nice • Follow the group and switch priorities to please everyone • Use language and ideas that are popular with the group
Teams	• Avoid conversations that could create friction • Conflate task and relationship conflict and avoid difficult conversations • Fall to the lowest common denominator to align with everyone, even if it leads to a watered-down solution
Organization	• Attempt to create "nice" cultures but ultimately lower performance standards • Overreliance on consensus-based decision-making • Fall into groupthink on big consequential decisions • Bury head in the sand when faced with significant challenges and smile through it all

*The descriptors of Likables are based on our experience with organizations and include items from the *Organizational Culture Inventory®* —copyrighted © by, and with the permission of, Human Synergistics International.

paradox.[11] This paradox describes what happens when each team member believes, mistakenly, that what he or she wants runs counter to the desires of the group. In an attempt to please everyone, the whole group agrees to a proposal that nobody actually wants because no one spoke up about what they actually wanted. This is akin to a family deciding to order pizza because they believe that other family members are tired of Chinese food when, in reality, everyone wants more lo mein. Everyone stumbles into a suboptimal outcome when this dynamic is at play.

The Interplay of Archetypes

No one person, team, or organization expresses just one archetype. Individuals and groups demonstrate a couple of primary or driving archetypes and a few minor archetypes that show up in reaction to specific situations. Usually, these unique combinations of archetypes create compounding dysfunctions. For example, I (Gaurav) have an unusual combination of archetypes: Competitor and Likable. For my entire adult life, I've had a deep need to be seen as supersmart or "the best." In groups, I hated admitting when I was wrong or not being the undisputed leader. At the same time, I also felt a need to be admired for my charming nature and ability to inspire.

Through many years of self-reflection, I have become increasingly conscious of these two tendencies and have learned how to manage them so that they don't create dysfunction in my teams and in my company. But old patterns die hard. When I lose that awareness, I spend inordinate energy creating and projecting a manufactured persona that does not align with my true self. I oscillate between these tendencies, Gaurav the Competitor and Gaurav the Likable. And this can confuse the heck out of people because my colleagues never know which version will show up. They invest time and resources in managing my ego instead of in more productive work.

Similarly, in many organizations, Passive/Defensive and Aggressive/Defensive behaviors reinforce each other and create a feedback loop of wasted energy. Two common patterns seen in these feedback loops are Aggressive leaders versus Passive employees and Aggressive leaders versus Aggressive leaders.

Aggressive Leaders Versus Passive Employees

This is one of the most common patterns that we observe. You can imagine how this can turn into a vicious, reinforcing cycle. Leaders, believing that their teams won't move or perform unless clearly directed through rules, top-down commands, and harsh punishments, impose their will on the company. Employees, believing that the will of the leaders always prevails, fall in line but remain passive. They don't put in discretionary effort out of a combination of burnout and fear that they will be punished for doing something that wasn't requested of them. This reinforces the leaders' belief that employees won't perform without direction. Motivated or emboldened employees either learn to become passive or leave, and leaders who fit this culture get hired and promoted, further entrenching this cycle in the company's culture.

Aggressive Leaders Versus Aggressive Leaders

Another pattern we often see in organizations is infighting across business units or functional groups. In these situations, leaders of different groups see the world as a zero-sum game and believe that the success of another leader is, by definition, a loss for them. We could call this the *Game of Thrones pattern*. Only one sovereign sits on the Iron Throne! Let the drama begin.

This is another self-reinforcing loop. A set of leaders with these tendencies will compete for resources, information, and recognition. They either find some success and believe that their strategy is working or they get frustrated that they're not winning and redouble their efforts. This causes other leaders in this ecosystem to adopt an aggressive stance or leave the company because it's not the environment in which they want to work. The cycle continues. In many of these situations, leaders and teams lack a shared sense of purpose, meaning, trust, and belonging.

Everyone is stuck in their individual orientation, and nobody pays attention to the bigger picture and how they can contribute to something beyond themselves or their narrow interests.

While these are the most common negative cycles we see, they aren't the only ones. Individual archetypes can clash to create vicious, draining dysfunction. Archetype conflicts aren't always limited to leader-team and leader-leader dynamics. Sometimes one employee will try to control a peer while another colleague avoids that employee. Likewise, these dynamics can play out at the team level or between the organization's leaders and other stakeholders (e.g., the board, regulatory groups, etc.). The key is to unfear each part of the organization. As the company breaks free of these archetypes, it can unlock higher levels of performance and well-being.

It's important to remember that teams and organizations that live in the fear archetypes are not bad people or systems and that they do not have bad intentions. Deep down, we all see ourselves as having positive values and wanting good things for ourselves and others. But we're often working with a complicated and often invisible relationship with our fears. Some of these unhealthy associations are cultural. Eastern cultures, like the one Gaurav comes from, tend to value tradition and community and are therefore more Passive/Defensive on average than Western cultures. Western cultures, like Mark's, value individuality and can be more Aggressive/Defensive. Even within the United States, though, you can see regional differences between, say, the Midwest and the Northeast in these behavioral tendencies. And some differences are industry based. For example, consultancies tend to be more Fault Finding as a general rule, sales organizations lean toward the Competitors, and government agencies skew toward Stickler tendencies. Many differences are simply based on our individual and collective stories of what we think of as strong leadership, high-performing teams, and effective organizations.

You may have recognized yourself, your team, and your organization in these archetypes. You may even have begun to understand the stories you tell yourself that keep you locked in these patterns of behavior. When we don't understand how these operate, it can feel like we are powerless. The dysfunctional traits of all these archetypes seem like the only options available to us. But in unfear reframing, you can choose a new role for each situation as it comes up. In the chapters that follow, we will give you practical advice on how you can use imagination and language to create new levels of effectiveness.

WORTH
THINKING
ABOUT

- Which of the eight fear archetypes or behavioral patterns do you tend to express? What about your team? Your organization?

- What do these patterns reveal about your values and priorities? What do they reveal about your fears and the stories you hold about them?

- How are these behavioral patterns and stories serving you? Your team? Your organization?

Part II
UNFEAR

4

Unfear Transformation

The Art and Science of Achieving and Sustaining Breakthrough Results

Several of the greatest innovations in business have come when people attempt to see things differently—to reframe and reimagine what sort of business they are in and what is possible in the world. For example, Netflix started as an alternative to Blockbuster. The company was somewhat successful, but it didn't really take off until it reimagined the business a few times, first as a streaming platform and then ultimately as an entertainment company. Most businesses are constantly doing some version of this reframing, looking at their strategy, market share, operational challenges, and so on and attempting to see these in a new light. While the reframing of external conditions can be very useful, it is not the only source of discovery and hardly the most powerful.

When we reframe our relationship with fear, we undergo a very similar process to reimagining how our business operates in the world. The key difference is that it is inside out and requires tremendous reflection and honesty as we question our internal beliefs and seek to shift them.

Although this process is deeply uncomfortable, it often leads to far more powerful results.

Let's consider Mohandas Gandhi, the main architect of the Indian freedom movement and the man who inspired Martin Luther King Jr., Nelson Mandela, and John Lewis. The way we interpret Gandhi's story is that he was able to help an entire nation reframe its relationship with fear. This reframe gave rise to a completely novel mass movement that energized millions of people to take risks, press on through difficult challenges, and deliver an extraordinary outcome: India's independence from colonial rule through a nonviolent revolution.

India in the 1920s was dominated by fear. The British still ruled and punished any act of "sedition" with immediate and violent force. The constant fear gave rise to two reactive, survival-oriented factions in Indian politics. The Aggressive/Defensive faction, the revolutionaries led by Chandrashekhar Azad and Bhagat Singh, wanted to fight fire with fire. They assassinated British agents and their sympathizers and attacked government buildings. The Passive/Defensive faction, led by the old guard of the Indian National Congress, believed that working within the bounds of the law of the colonial government would lead to more generosity and concessions from the British.

Gandhi offered a third way. He encouraged everyone to respond to British cruelty with creativity. They disobeyed onerous British laws but remained nonviolent. They didn't strike back out of fear, nor did they back down. One of his most famous actions in this vein was the 1930 Salt March. The British colonial government had prohibited Indians from harvesting or selling salt themselves. Instead, they had to buy the salt produced in India from British-approved companies and pay a salt tax to the colonial government.

In 1930, over the course of nearly a month, Gandhi and 78 volunteers marched 388 kilometers from Ahmedabad to Dandi, Gujarat. They had a stated aim of breaking the law by harvesting salt themselves. Along the way, Gandhi spoke to huge crowds. Thousands of Indians joined him in Dandi. Gandhi symbolically harvested and distributed the salt himself, and the British arrested him and many other leaders of the movement. The movement went ahead without the arrested leaders, with new people stepping in to lead the next planned action, the picketing of the Dharasana Salt Works on May 21, 1930. This is how Miller Webb of United Press, a famous American journalist, described the incident:[1]

> In complete silence the Gandhi men drew up and halted a hundred yards from the stockade. A picket column advanced from the crowd, waded the ditches and approached the barbed wire stockade. . . . At a word of command, scores of native policemen rushed upon the advancing marchers and rained blows on their heads with their steel-shot lathis [long bamboo sticks]. Not one of the marchers even raised an arm to fend off blows. They went down like tenpins. From where I stood I heard the sickening whack of the clubs on unprotected skulls. . . . Those struck down fell sprawling, unconscious or writhing with fractured skulls or broken shoulders.

By the time the protest was over, 2 people were dead and 300 or more protestors had been beaten, many severely injured. It showed Indians that the British could use violence to hurt their bodies but had no ability to control their response. The British, in contrast, could no longer justify using violence as a way to suppress nonviolence from the other side. Furthermore, Webb's words echoed around the world, leading to several nations questioning British tactics in India.

This campaign was one of Gandhi's most successful at loosening the British hold on India. Eventually, Gandhi went to London to negotiate Britain's eventual departure from India. This was a man Winston Churchill once described as "a seditious Middle Temple lawyer, now posing as a fakir of a type well known in the East, striding half-naked up the steps of the Vice-regal palace . . . to parley on equal terms with the representative of the King-Emperor."

The "easy" route would have been to stick with the old Aggressive/ Defensive and Passive/Defensive strategies. But Gandhi got a whole country to reframe its relationship with fear, to see that the people had other choices, and to win their independence.

We all have the same power and potential. We can lead ourselves and our organizations to tremendous, profound new successes. It has very little to do with size and financial position and nothing to do with how large the adversity is. It has everything to do with our willingness to reframe our relationship with fear and inspire our organizations to do the same. Here is how to make this happen.

Reframing Our Relationship with Fear

Think about an event or period in your life that led to significant learning or growth. It could be anything—a move to another country, a job loss, a divorce, or a surprising position of responsibility. Once you have this event in mind, write down the ways you changed and grew because of that experience.

Next, recall how you felt when you first encountered this event— when you got the news that you needed to move, when you received the divorce papers, or when you learned of your promotion. What emotions did you experience? Was it easy or did you feel fear? Did you struggle to get to where you are today?

Chances are that you felt some fear as you faced that moment of learning and growth. This is exactly what happened to me (Gaurav) when I entered one of the most profound periods of growth in my life. In 2006, my manager at McKinsey told me that the company found my performance inadequate and that I had to leave the firm within two months. I can remember that moment like it was yesterday—all my fears and insecurities came bursting to the fore. I was not good enough. I was a failure. How was I going to provide for my family? I should have worked harder. I wasn't as smart as my colleagues. And so on.

It took me a week before I could even talk about it to anyone. When I finally did talk about it, I alternated between righteous anger and self-pity. I blamed my manager for not seeing my value because of his "old school" point of view. I felt undermined by my peers on my team and cursed anyone I could think of. I disproved to myself everything in the review and found countless examples of how my reviewers were inferior to me.

This was a defining moment in my life. It forced me to figure out who I was and actively define the unique contribution I wanted to make to the world. I had to choose: Would I continue to pretend to be someone I was not, to try to fit in and survive at a company that did not value my contribution? Or would I step into my uniqueness and not base my self-esteem on the approval of others?

For a few years before this, I had been learning about my relationship with fear and how it impacted my life. This was the first time that I had to apply those lessons in such a dramatic and personal context, and I developed a two-part routine. Whenever I felt fear, I forced myself to pause, engage my prefrontal cortex, notice my stories about fear, and let them go. Then, every day, I would meditate and pose two questions to myself: Why have I created this current state of affairs? What can I learn from it?

Through this process of reflection, I discovered my true voice. I deepened my understanding of fear—how it can serve as a cue to growth and how to learn to transform my relationship with it. I learned how to become resilient in the face of adversity and, more important, how to help others do the same. Interestingly, it also led me to have a dialogue with my manager at McKinsey about how I could contribute to the firm by doing what I did best. We realized that it would benefit us both to have me continue working at McKinsey, and I spent four more years there before I decided to start my own company.

The point is simple: Fear is neither good nor bad. It is merely an emotion you feel when you get an outcome that is different from what you expect. The story we create about fear matters more than the fear itself. We control those stories and can craft either a negative one of doom and gloom or see fear as a cue for growth. When we are able to do the latter, fear becomes a path that leads us to a better future.

> *The story we create about fear matters more than the fear itself. We control those stories and can craft either a negative one of doom and gloom or one that sees fear as a cue for growth.*

This realization and reframe must happen before any other part of the unfear transformation. Unfortunately, because of our survival orientation, we default to telling defensive stories around fear. This is what I did initially, which left me mired in pain and helplessness. I only grew from the experience when I realized that the fear I was feeling highlighted an opportunity for me to stop measuring my worth in terms of success at McKinsey. After that, I stepped with more purpose into my real contribution to the world. The same holds true at an organizational level. Anything that causes widespread fear in an organization—a market shift, a product recall, an economic downturn—presents an opportunity for learning and growth.

Our superpowers of imagination and language allow us to design our future. When we tell a defensive or threatening story about fear, we fall into the fear archetypes, and those behaviors shape our future. When we create a story of possibility and view fear as a cue for learning, we can change, transform, and adopt more effective behaviors. Neither of the two stories is wrong. They can both be true. But they lead to fundamentally different future outcomes. One keeps us stuck, whereas the other opens the path to learning and growth. We all hold the keys to both doors.

The Wise Club: The Unfear Archetypes

Once we reframe our relationship with fear, we can begin the transformation process that will eventually lead us to the unfear archetypes. Both the fear and unfear archetypes experience fear. The key difference is the story they tell themselves about that fear. When we are in the fear archetypes, we act in dysfunctional ways because we believe that it is the only choice. In the unfear archetypes, however, we recognize that fear is a cue for learning and growth and that we can choose how we respond to it. Like the fear archetypes, we developed the unfear archetypes inspired by the work of Dr. Robert Cooke and his organization, Human Synergistics.[2] (See the Appendix for more detail on Human Synergistics' Styles Inventory Circumplex and surveys, and how the Unfear Archetypes relates to and builds on them.)

> *Both the fear and unfear archetypes experience fear. The key difference is the story they tell themselves about that fear.*

Individuals who demonstrate the unfear archetypes exhibit self-enhancing or growth tendencies that contribute to greater levels of personal satisfaction and well-being. They perform at a high level and can work well with almost any team. Unfear organizations believe that investing in people will help ensure their long-term success. They allow employees to express themselves in their work—to test, experiment, and learn from both successes and failures. They place a strong emphasis on transparency and communication and encourage people to get to know their colleagues as people instead of just as roles or objects to be used or overcome. Let's explore the four unfear archetypes (Figure 4.1).

FIGURE 4.1   Unfear archetypes

 # Seekers

Seekers[3] strive for self- and collective improvement. They seek to maximize their potential. They don't do this in a competitive or destructive manner but combine this yearning for self-improvement with an acceptance of others. They strive *with* not *over* others. They recognize that admitting when they don't know something propels individual and collective learning. They create safety to speak up and show up with curiosity. They take calculated risks to create better outcomes. They tend to develop innovative, unique solutions to difficult problems. This archetype allows for the free flow of ideas and creates an infectious positive energy, even in the face of challenges. Organizations that display this archetype nurture vulnerability, which allows employees to deal with change effectively and take the risks that lead to breakthrough solutions.

For much of its early years, Google exemplified the Seeker culture. The company intentionally hired people who fit the Seeker archetype: highly intelligent, curious, and conscientious individuals who were comfortable with ambiguity and change.[4] The company had several programs that entrenched its Seeker culture, including weekly all-hands meetings where company leadership would share successes and failures in an unscripted way and field questions from employees. As part of these all-hands meetings, the company would also have employees vote on improvement ideas and volunteer to help make them happen. This ritual got employees actively engaged in innovation and improvement. The transparency also displayed and built trust. In the latter half of the 2010s, there were some rumblings that Google had strayed from its Seeker roots.[5] Whether or not this is true, the early culture the company built, the culture that in many ways fueled the company's rise, was a quintessential example of a Seeker culture.

One of our clients is a healthcare payor for underserved communities in New York City. This, as you might imagine, is a challenging mission and industry. The organization and its employees face significant business and human challenges to run a successful company and make a meaningful difference. People care deeply about what they do and have a highly constrained budget to get it all done. It is exactly the kind of environment where fear might run rampant. When we first met the CEO, that was exactly what was happening. He had been one of the earliest employees of the company, and he cared deeply about its success. Driven by his passion to make a difference and burdened by a feeling that it was all up to him, the CEO tended to lead with more Aggressive/Defensive behaviors, in particular the Fault Finder archetype.

He had a strong Seeker side to him, although he rarely expressed it. Early in our conversations, to his great delight, he recognized these two conflicting archetypes within him. We worked with the CEO on this, and he eagerly jumped into the work. He learned to move away from his Fault Finder tendencies. In situations where it would be easy for him to blame others, he now seeks to understand how he has contributed to the problem and what he needs to do differently to create a better outcome. He constantly uses the refrain, "Feeling into my discomfort and pain."

This is what Seekers do. They lean into their own fear and discomfort to see what they need to shift to be more effective. Through this behavior, the CEO has significantly improved the quality of his relationships and the effectiveness of the entire organization.

Seekers* Archetype Profile

Leaders	• Voracious problem solvers and creators of new ideas and solutions • Great at questioning assumptions and beliefs without making people wrong • Trust their intuition and develop long-term realistic goals • Encourage teams to self-organize • Have a zest for life that is contagious
Employees	• Pursue self-development • Do not stew in guilt or worry • Respect traditions, but do not feel bound to them • Desire to experience things directly • Are very curious
Teams	• Look for solutions rather than point out mistakes of other groups • Collaborate and share ideas to come up with even better solutions • Are willing to ask for help and confidently say "I don't know" as a path to learning
Organization	• Value quality over quantity • Embrace and adapt to change • Take a systems view and include stakeholders outside the organization, (e.g., customers, suppliers, communities, and even competitors) when exploring solutions • Design learning routines and habits to foster regular problem solving, innovation, and continuous improvement • Have feelings of spontaneity • Encourage personal integrity

*The descriptors of Seekers are based on our experience with organizations and include items from the *Organizational Culture Inventory*® —copyrighted © by, and with the permission of, Human Synergistics International.

Coaches

Coaches[6] are people builders, teachers, and mentors. Unlike Fault Finders, who see their role as pointing out other people's faults, or Likables, who withhold feedback to avoid creating distress, Coaches build the capabilities and confidence of other people with care and compassion. Coaches have mastered the ability to simultaneously express how much they care while providing direct feedback. These individuals strive to create a nurturing environment that inspires self-development and high performance. They also take time to help others reframe their relationship with fear. Coaches focus on patterns that need to shift in others and figure out how best to show up to make that happen. The Coach culture allows for growth and learning without the caustic effects of excessive judgment. The Coach archetype creates a virtuous cycle in which the organization attracts exceptional talent and nurtures and develops that talent for leadership, which, in turn, attracts more talent.

One of my (Gaurav's) most important mentors embodied all the unfear archetypes, and he was an incredible coach. This man, Michael Rennie, was my mentor at McKinsey, and he inspired me to work on human potential and cultural transformation. I always knew that he had my back, even in the moments when he gave me difficult feedback. One such moment, which had a massive impact on my career, came when I had just moved back from South Africa to work with him in New York. By the time I arrived, Michael had been out of the office for a few months because of illness, and I felt that I had no support in the New York office. So I drove all the way to Michael's house in Amish country in rural Pennsylvania to complain to him. Michael listened to everything I had to say and then told me, "Gaurav, you have tremendous potential, and I believe in you. But you are getting in your own way."

I was shocked and wondered if he'd heard a word of what I'd said about how unfair the office had been. He saw the shock on my face and smiled. Then he looked directly at me and, with great care, told me that I was giving up my power through all my complaining. He reminded me that it is difficult to create change. He invited me to step into my power to bring about change and to stop letting other people become excuses for not doing so. I listened to him, and he supported me while I worked to figure out my path.

Isao Yoshino, a visionary leader at Toyota, once said, "My role as a leader was to help others develop themselves." This sentiment perfectly captures the Coach culture. In organizations with a strong Coach culture, managers aim to build the skills and confidence of employees to solve their own problems and confidently ask for help when they need it.

In her book, *Learning to LEAD, Leading to LEARN*,[7] Katie Anderson documents the culture of Toyota through the eyes and ears of Yoshino. Toyota lets their employees solve problems themselves, instead of providing the answers for them. Company leaders believe that developing their people produces better and more sustainable results than taking shortcuts.

A Coach culture doesn't just mean coaching conversations. Organizations can build systems that make the development of others a natural part of doing business. To facilitate this coaching, Toyota has developed a wide set of practices. One is "going to the *gemba*," or "going to where the work is done." It allows Coaches to get a sense of the real, specific challenges that employees face in their environment so that they can best guide the employees in the pursuit of their goals. This also applies to the "coachee." To better think through a problem, coachees are encouraged to "go and see" to learn more about the issue directly rather than making too many assumptions.

A linked practice to this is the *andon*, or "signal," cord. Essentially, if frontline employees can't resolve an issue within a certain amount of time, they are encouraged to pull the *andon* cord, which tells the supervisor that they are struggling and need some assistance. They then stop or slow down the manufacturing line so that the manager can work with the employees to solve the issue. They don't punish employees for pulling this cord, even though it is costly to slow down the line. They think that it is more valuable to make sure that the work is done right and to develop the skills of the employees instead of allowing subpar outputs to

Coaches* Archetype Profile

Leaders	• Are deeply concerned about other people and their growth • Work to mentor and support others in their self-improvement • Appreciate when people raise their hand to ask questions or request support and help • Exhibit candor paired with deep care for individuals (e.g., Radical Candor)
Employees	• Appreciate people's strengths and believe in their potential • Commit to relationships beyond superficial niceties • Do not see development as a purely hierarchical concept and therefore give/receive feedback to/from peers • Ask for help or support when needed • Listen deeply and consistently
Teams	• Leverage individual strengths to create outcomes greater than the sum of the parts • Share the credit and blame and work to improve each other
Organization	• View the primary role of management as people development • Show concern for the needs of its members • Exhibit high employee satisfaction and deep commitment to the organization • Celebrate problems or challenges as a chance to learn and develop • Focus on constructive dialogue and creative conflict

*The descriptors of Coaches are based on our experience with organizations and include items from the *Organizational Culture Inventory®* —copyrighted © by, and with the permission of, Human Synergistics International.

pass through the facility. This is a practical tool but also a symbolic one. Raising your hand to say, "I have an issue, and I need help" is accepted and celebrated, even when it feels inconvenient in the moment. This same philosophy works in an office setting, but instead of pulling a literal cord, employees can take the initiative to either raise their hand or send an email to request help.

Trust Builders

Trust Builders[8] are phenomenal team players. They create groups that energetically and effectively coordinate their actions to achieve meaningful shared goals. They build teams that reframe their relationship with fear and can engage in difficult conversations with skill. They create cross-silo collaboration and build effective, trust-based networks of people with common interests and passions. They demonstrate strong interpersonal skills and use genuine praise to motivate others. Trust Builders see patterns in team dysfunction that they help shift.

Organizations with strong Trust Builder cultures facilitate open communication, coordination, and learning routines that allow teams to work together effectively. Trust Builders create psychological safety within the organization by ensuring that everyone feels respected and heard. This allows them to contribute to their fullest.

One of our other clients is a healthcare provider for underserved populations. During the 2010s, policy decisions at every level of government dramatically reduced funding for such organizations, which forced a number of them to shut down or seek a merger. Our client was merging with a larger organization, and the client asked us to coach one of the organization's executives, whom we will call Charlotte. Charlotte was working with her counterpart on the other side of the deal to ensure the merger's success. The business case for the merger was sound, but the two leadership teams disagreed about the vision for the future of the organization and over what roles each leader would play after the deal. This shattered the trust between the two sides. Charlotte and her counterpart suddenly needed not only to manage the technical details of the deal but also to get the workforces of both companies on board.

Instead of collapsing under the pressure of the situation, Charlotte used her Trust-Building skills and facilitated open dialogue within and across the two leadership teams about their fears and concerns. She then worked individually with key leaders to help them see the benefit of the merger for them and, more important, for the population they served.

Then, in an ultimate test, the CEO of her own organization quit. This threw the whole deal into jeopardy, and the rest of Charlotte's executive team seemed close to walking away. She facilitated negotiations between her executive team and their peers in the other organization and ensured that the deal had mutually beneficial terms that would retain key leaders. It has been over a year since the merger, and the two organizations are successfully charting a path forward. Charlotte is an important leader on the new executive team who ensures that the two legacy organizations work together harmoniously.

A Trust Builder organization par excellence might be Menlo Innovations, the development company run by CEO and cofounder Rich Sheridan. In describing his management philosophy, Sheridan said, "If we can pump the fear out of the room and get people trusting each other enough, then you start to get that collaboration and teamwork." Although we might argue that you can never just pump the fear out, we agree with him. This is exactly what Trust Builders do. They reduce fear and help people respond to whatever fear still exists with resilience and by coming together in common cause. Sheridan's book, *Joy, Inc.: How We Built a Workplace People Love*,[9] is a master class in trust and team building, and we highly recommend it. For our purposes, we highlight two keys to a Trust Builder culture that his book provides.

First, Sheridan and the Menlo management team believe that if people find joy in what they do, they'll naturally work hard and well, without much supervision and micromanagement. Part of that joy comes from a feeling of trust and inclusion and a belief that everyone's voices will be heard. Sheridan and Menlo managers manifest this belief in several ways: an open-plan workplace, a nonhierarchical organizational structure, soliciting input from the whole office on hiring decisions, and flexible working arrangements that, for example, allow employees to bring their dogs and babies (which, for some people, are the same thing) to work.

Second, Menlo management extends the network of trust beyond the walls of the company to include its customers. They treat customers

Trust Builders* Archetype Profile

Leaders	• Are well-liked by both subordinates and coworkers
	• Emphasize teamwork and value subordinates who work well with each other
	• See their role as enablers of teamwork rather than controllers of team activity
	• Have a willingness to openly share feelings and thoughts
Employees	• Build meaningful relationships
	• Have strong interpersonal skills
	• Emphasize the well-being of all team members
Teams	• Celebrate successes and use these to move work forward
	• Work effectively across silos
	• Embrace customers and suppliers and see them as part of their team
Organization	• Create a culture of cooperation and support rather than blame and avoidance
	• Create processes and structures that foster teamwork and collaboration across whole value chains
	• Embrace customers, suppliers, and communities rather than seeing them as "other"
	• Emphasize group satisfaction and build respect for all members
	• Promote an environment of trust which ensures organizations surface and solve tough challenges rather than keep them hidden

* The descriptors of Trust Builders are based on our experience with organizations and include items from the *Organizational Culture Inventory®* —copyrighted © by, and with the permission of, Human Synergistics International.

as an essential part of the software delivery teams. Through a ritual called "Show&Tell," they involve customers in the weekly working rhythm. During Show&Tell, customers come in and demonstrate to the software team how the company's product is working (or not). This turns the tables on the development team. Rather than them "presenting" the product to customers, they have to sit and watch while customers use the product in front of them. Any successes, issues, or strong emotions quickly become apparent. This dynamic creates deep trust and rapport between both the delivery team and the customers. The team can respond directly to the customers' needs and wants. Trust grows. Everyone wins.

Achievers

Achievers[10] set bold yet achievable goals and apply themselves and the organization to them. They do so without wasting time and energy in perfectionism or misplaced competition. They create effective learning routines and disciplines within the organization. They do not shy away from the hard work needed to achieve meaningful goals. Achievers do not hesitate to act on knowledge that will improve things. They see patterns in the breakdown of learning routines and create new pathways to address them.

SpaceX, founded by Elon Musk in 2002 on the assumption that the cost of launching rockets into space could be reduced by a factor of 10, exemplifies the Achiever culture. Our sense is that the SpaceX skews in the unfear direction, based on how employees describe the culture. Writing in *Forbes*, Josh Boehm, a former leader of software quality assurance at SpaceX, reflected on the long hours he put in this way: "I loved my work and saw the value I was bringing to the team. I technically reported to the CIO, but was essentially self-managed like many others there at the time."[11]

The way the company has continued to achieve, even in the face of notable challenges, also indicates a strong Achiever orientation. The company bounces back stronger from setbacks instead of collapsing into blame and total risk aversion. In 2019, a test version of SpaceX's Crew Dragon space capsule exploded during a ground test in Florida. After intensive investigations with NASA, the company found the source of the failure and fixed it. On May 30, 2020, SpaceX successfully launched two astronauts into space in the Crew Dragon spacecraft named *Endeavour*, atop a Falcon 9 rocket. *Endeavour* later docked with the International

Space Station. SpaceX was the first private company to accomplish such a feat. Earlier failures were simply a part of this later success.

To embody the Achiever culture, however, you don't need all the glitz and glam of Space X. An Achiever has a can-do attitude in the face of any task or challenge. Few people I (Mark) know exemplify the Achiever mindset more than the Navy Seabees. There are few jobs less glamorous, yet while I served with the Seabees, I was consistently impressed by their dedication and hard work. Once, a utilities man (a plumber and heating, ventilation, and air conditioning specialist) in my unit literally jumped into feces to unclog the old pipes at a military base in Kuwait. Given the dirty nature of the job, I was concerned about his morale. But he popped out of that hole with a huge smile on his face. When I asked if it was an awful experience, he said something like, "Nah, I'm glad I did that. Those toilets need to work!"

The Seabees aren't what most people imagine when they think about important military operational work. But almost everyone in the military knows just how vital they are. These men and women take on all sorts of projects that improve the functioning and welfare of military personnel, including building and operating camps, moving gear ashore for the Army and Marines, running construction projects in war zones, and providing humanitarian relief. Through all the work, they maintain a cheery can-do spirit—even when they are literally wading in shit. This is the Achiever mindset—taking on the hard, dirty work without the need for any special recognition. The hard work itself is the reward.

A mature Achiever organization builds an environment in which performance can be decoupled from reactive fear-based behavior and can coexist with employee well-being.

Achievers* Archetype Profile

Leaders	• Do not focus on just the results but also process and learning routines needed to sustain the results
	• Encourage subordinates to give their best on every project
	• Set stretch but realistic performance goals
	• Engage subordinates in dialogue about goals and methods
Employees	• Focus on achieving a high standard of excellence
	• Tend to focus on understanding root causes and causalities to drive more effective performance
Teams	• Set and maintain high standards for their processes and expected outcomes
	• Work hard without feeling stressed or drained
	• See challenges as invigorating
	• Approach problems with curiosity and openness
Organization	• Inspire people in the organization to stretch and achieve meaningful outcomes; have a purpose that extends beyond just profit to create meaningful contribution to the world
	• Establish effective plans to reach business objectives and pursue them with enthusiasm
	• Value members who take initiative to set and accomplish lofty but achievable goals
	• See missed goals as opportunities for learning and growth; problems are celebrated as learning moments
	• Emphasize the development and maintenance of processes and routines that lead to good outcomes, rather than the outcomes themselves

*The descriptors of Achievers are based on our experience with organizations and include items from the *Organizational Culture Inventory®* by Robert A. Cooke and J. Clayton Lafferty (1987). Copyright © Human Synergistics International. All Rights Reserved. Used by Permission.

No individual, team, or organization has only the unfear or fear archetypes. In fact, these archetypes are not fixed. Through active choice and deliberate practice, any individual, team, or organization can consciously step into (and out of) the archetypes most appropriate for creating business performance and employee well-being in different business environments.

Inside-Out: How to Ignite an Unfear Transformation

It is not enough to merely recognize that fear indicates an opportunity for growth. We need to know how to actually grow and transform in a way that allows us to achieve the results we desire and to become unfear individuals, teams, and organizations. This process—the actual transformation—is the hard part. As we mentioned in Chapter 2, our habits are literally hardwired into our brains, and it takes sustained effort to rewire them. On an organizational level, two-thirds of all transformation efforts fail to achieve their goals of sustained long-term top- and bottom-line growth and/or high levels of employee engagement. What is perhaps the most jarring about this figure is the fact that it has barely changed over time. Two-thirds of transformation efforts failed in 1996, as John Kotter detailed in his seminal book, *Leading Change*,[12] and according to a 2015 survey from the McKinsey Global Institute, two-thirds still fail now.[13]

The fact that the figure has stayed consistent, even as our understanding of and investment in transformation have increased, indicates that most of these efforts are missing an essential element: a deep understanding of what transformation actually requires. In our experience, most transformation efforts fail because they make cosmetic improvements instead of powering *true* transformation.

If we were to ask you to give us a definition of the word *transformation*, what would your response be? Most people would say that transformation is "significant change" or "a large change in the way an organization behaves to achieve dramatically better results." But this doesn't go deep enough. From our years of experience, we have found that transformation efforts, both for individuals and for organizations, work best when they seek a *fundamental* change—a metamorphosis. In other words, a true transformation turns a caterpillar into a butterfly instead of outfitting a caterpillar with wings. A true transformation, a metamorphosis, has two characteristics that a cosmetic change lacks.

First, a transformation occurs in the DNA of an organism. What is the DNA of an organization? Is it the profit and loss? The office buildings? The machinery? The computers? The data servers? The systems and processes? Of course not. The DNA is the *people*. Remove the people, and you do not have an organization. This means that to create a true transformation in an organization, we first need to create a transformation among the people. We need to move away from how most people view transformational efforts, which start by changing the organization and its systems and hoping that those changes alter the teams and the individuals. We must instead start with the individual (Figure 4.2).

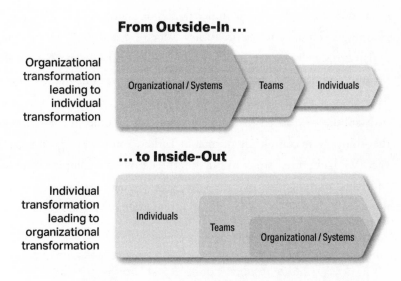

FIGURE 4.2   Inside-out transformation

Simply put, organizations do not transform; *individuals* do. When a critical mass of individuals transforms, then the organization transforms.

Second, metamorphosis doesn't just change our behavior but also the root perspective through which we experience life. A butterfly in the air has a fundamentally different perspective than a caterpillar crawling on a leaf. As human beings, transformation requires us to re-create our mental models. We must shift the perspective from which we experience and respond to ourselves, others, and situations.

> *Organizations do not transform; individuals do. When a critical mass of individuals transforms, then the organization transforms.*

Despite what many of us want to believe, we are not objective observers in an objective world. We live in an *interpretive* world. We each see things with our unique filter or lens, which constantly alters the course of our actions in ways we rarely understand. For example, in 2019, we were planning a company retreat in Turkey. When we saw news reports of the Syrian crisis spilling over into Turkey, we decided to go somewhere else because we imagined that Turkey was dangerous and in complete chaos. This was our perspective. When we spoke with a close friend who lives in Istanbul, we realized that our view was hardly objective. He told us that things were completely normal in Turkey, and it was a great time to visit. We had gotten stuck in our interpretation of a complex situation and failed to remember that the knowledge we had was incomplete and not fully accurate. We got caught up in the drama of a good story.

> *Metamorphosis doesn't just change our behavior but also the root perspective through which we experience life. Transformation requires us to recreate our mental models.*

The way we see and interpret things influences the actions we take. This is because the way we understand and frame a particular situation creates a *unique starting-point set of possibilities* and eliminates others. This is the process that plays out whenever a company gets so stuck in its thinking that it misses an opportunity, and a competitor innovates and disrupts the company's situation. The graveyard of business is littered with such examples—Blockbuster, BlackBerry, and so on.

To experience a true unfear transformation, the process must begin from the inside out. Start at the most basic level, with the DNA of the organization, and focus on transforming individuals. Only then can you start shifting culture at the team and organizational levels. An inside-out transformation process never quite ends. We constantly feel the pull of fear and the dysfunctional fear-based behavioral archetypes. We constantly desire better and more substantive results. As we learn to overcome certain dysfunctional stories about fear, new ones might emerge. As our circumstances change, new fears will reveal themselves. This is as true for teams and organizations as it is for individuals. As teams overcome certain challenges, new ones arise. As organizations grow, new layers of complexity and new issues present themselves. The fear returns to cue yet more learning. Ultimately, this is the core of an unfear transformation: learning.

> *An unfear transformation is an*
> *inside-out transformation.*

In an unfear transformation, we recognize fear as an invitation to learn, and we accept that invitation. We break learning down into two levels. The first is *transformational* learning. This has to do with our mindsets, our assumptions, and our beliefs. The second is *action* learning, which is comprised of all the external actions that result from the shift in our mindsets.

Transformational Learning

Transformational learning happens when we change the root perspective from which we make sense of ourselves, others, and the world. Changing our mindsets changes how we see and enables us to understand the world in an entirely new way. When Newton observed the apple falling, he realized that there is a force that pulls everything down toward Earth in predictable ways, and he discovered gravity. We also go through events that cause transformational learning in our personal lives all the time. For example, when I (Mark) held my first-born daughter, my entire root perspective changed. Up to that point in my life, I was responsible only for myself, my own survival and well-being. When I had a child, I suddenly was responsible for another human being. That fundamentally changed how I viewed myself, the world, my priorities, and the options that were available to me. The beautiful thing about human beings is that we do not have to wait for an event to trigger a mindset shift. By leveraging our superpowers of language and imagination, we can change our own mindsets and beliefs.

This transformational learning also plays out in the business world regularly. For example, one of our team members tells a great story about a leader she was coaching. The leader told her that she was struggling because no matter the job, she always had a boss from hell. Each time she found a job that she thought she liked, it turned out that her boss was impossible to collaborate with. So she went from job to job, unsatisfied. Then her coach asked, "In all those situations, what was the one constant?"

The answer, of course, was her. In that moment, the leader recognized that in all of her previous jobs, she'd been showing up in a dysfunctional way. From there, a whole new set of possibilities, for ways that she could change and grow, became apparent.

Transformational learning also takes place at the team and organizational levels—at the level of collective mindsets or shared mental models. For example, one of our clients, a nonprofit organization, asked us to help it with a process redesign effort for an operational team. During our initial interviews, we discovered that the problem ran far deeper than any process redesign could fix.

Each functional group had dramatically different goals. The business development team wanted more corporate partnerships and sales and thought that it could achieve this only by bending to the whim of each corporate partner. The operations people, out of concern for employees' sky-rocketing stress, wanted less complexity and more efficiency in processing customer and partner requests. But they believed that they couldn't question the important work of the business development team. The product development folks were overwhelmed by the backlog of fixes they had to make to tailor what they offered to each new corporate partner and struggled to communicate the logic of their prioritization choices.

Instead of redesigning the processes of the operations team, we invited leaders (including frontline employees) from each of the departments to a value-stream-mapping workshop. During the workshop, we helped each group articulate its implicit stories and assumptions. This organization exhibited strong Avoider and Likable tendencies. In the face of fear and stress, the implicit assumption that people and teams held was that they couldn't openly question each other. To do so would challenge their nice atmosphere. But underneath the calm veneer, people carried a lot of pent-up stress and frustration.

In the course of our work with these teams, we helped team members understand and shift their collective beliefs behind the patterns of behavior that led to this stress and underperformance. The business development team realized that it didn't need to cave to every demand of the corporate partners. Team members started to believe (and later, in practice, proved) that they could meet their partners' needs by customizing features only occasionally. The operations team learned to ask for help, without apologizing for it, when team members felt overwhelmed. The product team learned that it could set clear priorities and say no at times without upsetting other teams.

At the end of one of our initial workshops, a member of the operations team broke down in tears of joy and relief. She told her team, "Thank you! After so many years, I finally feel I can speak up and be heard. Now you understand what I've been dealing with this whole time!"

This is the power of transformational learning. Everyone in the organization had gone years without realizing that they held certain mindsets and that they could be explored and fundamentally changed. This organization learned that its people could challenge each other with respect—and everyone was better for it. Once we cleared up the ways in which the mindsets and assumptions of individuals were impacting performance, we could move on to the actual process redesign, which falls under the category of action learning.

Action Learning

We can't simply change our mindsets, see new opportunities, and expect success. We need to take actual steps to translate our intangible mindsets into tangible success. We call the skills needed to take these steps *action learning*. Action learning covers a huge range of skills—functional, technical, leadership and management, analytical, and so on. Essentially, action learning covers any skill that you can improve without a fundamental change in perspective. Of course, a change in perspective can and will change how you practice any of these skills, but you can deepen your mastery of these skills without changing your perspective. You can learn how to write computer code, adopt new advertising or management techniques, and deepen your mastery of statistical analysis without a fundamental change in perspective. However, action learning alone can go only so far. It must be paired with transformational learning to create sustainable, breakthrough results.

Our purpose in this book isn't to catalog everything that you can possibly learn. Nor is it to describe every action you can take to unfear yourself, your team, and your organization. Instead, we focus on the actions you can take that will support the specific, key mindset shifts that allow for an unfear transformation. More often than not, these actions will help you to live the mindset changes that you've made. But they will also help to move you toward your desired results.

For the most part, the actions that support the mindset shifts necessary to unfear yourself and the actions we cover in this book are conversations. Although people usually think of talking and acting as opposites, the reality is that for most leaders, most of what they do is have and convene conversations that coordinate others' actions.

It is the quality of the conversations that we have that, in many ways, determines our ability to unfear. Our internal conversations allow us as individuals to reframe our relationship with fear, while our external conversations allow us to surface the fear and mindsets that might be holding us back as a team and as an organization. In other words, we show you how to use action learning as a delivery mechanism for transformational learning rather than as a replacement for it. In our experience, this is how organizations and individuals achieve sustained breakthrough performance. To return to the example of the nonprofit organization, once the members realized how their mindsets were holding them back, we helped them develop the skills that would allow them to actually collaborate across silos. We worked on the habits and practices that would make it easier for them to build trust, to have difficult conversations in an effective manner, and to share information and ideas across teams.

When faced with a gap between their current and desired results, most individuals, teams, and organization respond by taking new actions. Depending on our current mindsets, though, we'll only see a limited set of possible actions for which we're already conditioned by our mindsets. In our example, the nonprofit felt like it just needed to redesign a process to solve their problem. They had a limited view of what was possible, but it made sense from their current mindset.

Access the type of learning that is truly needed for your situation. In particular, if you're stuck in the fear archetypes, more actions taken from your current mindset likely won't work. You'll need to shift your mindset first and then, from your new vantage point, try new actions that lead you to better results (Figure 4.3).

When people combine transformational and action learning, it can lead to remarkable results. A famous example of this was the NUMMI plant owned by General Motors (GM). In the 1980s, this was a notorious car manufacturing plant. The employees didn't care, they drank on the job,

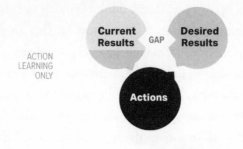

FIGURE 4.3   Shift mindsets first

and they even sabotaged products by doing things like placing empty beer bottles inside the car door so that they would rattle while the customer drove around. GM couldn't figure out how to transform the culture of their whole company and this plant in particular. At the same time, Toyota was looking to get a foothold in the American market, and the company needed a site to manufacture its vehicles. GM and Toyota struck a partnership deal whereby GM would turn over control of the NUMMI plant to Toyota.

Toyota kept 85 percent of the workforce and implemented the Toyota Production System (TPS). TPS leverages a mix of transformational and action learning. It requires workers to change their mindsets, connect to a higher sense of purpose, and view themselves as vital members of the organization. It compels them to adopt a mindset of continuous evolution, in which everyone, from the frontline to senior executives, looks for ways to improve the system. And Toyota combined this approach with concrete actions, such as "going to *gemba*" that we mentioned earlier. The results were spectacular. Virtually overnight, the plant began to outperform most other GM plants.

Unfortunately, most people fail to combine action learning with transformational learning because transformational learning is more difficult to measure in terms of dollars and cents. This is what happened with just about every American car manufacturer after the success of the NUMMI plant. Most major American car companies tried to implement TPS, but they didn't understand the role that mindsets and transformational learning played in that system. They thought it was all about the actions and implemented those but still saw lackluster results and a sluggish company culture.

True transformation isn't possible without the combination of transformational learning and action learning. Together they form our model for creating unfear individuals, teams, and organizations (Figure 4.4).

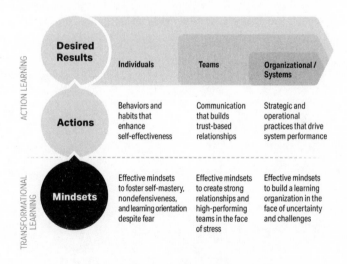

FIGURE 4.4   Summary of model

In Chapter 5, we describe in detail the attributes of the unfear individual and provide the transformational and action learning steps that you can take to unfear yourself.

WORTH THINKING ABOUT

- Which of the four unfear archetypes or behavioral patterns do you tend to express? What about your team? Your organization?

- Which of these unfear archetypes would you like to adopt for yourself? Your team? Your organization?

- What mindset shifts might be required to express these unfear archetypes more consistently for yourself? Your team? Your organization?

- What is the upside of experiencing fear?

5

The Unfear Individual
Freeing the Angel in the Stone

F ar too many organizations treat individuals as cogs in a machine— as a resource, something to be leveraged and disposed of. Because of this, too often they also view individuals as fixed. People are who they are, and they can each fill a specific role or function. When, for whatever reason, they can no longer perform that role or that role is no longer necessary, the company gets rid of them. In seeing individuals as cogs, companies treat them as replaceable, and they respond to each new challenge or shift in the business environment by changing personnel. This belief and the accompanying practices constitute one of the most powerful blocks to sustainable organizational transformation. It is far better—and more efficient—to create an organization filled with unfear individuals—people who work creatively, who find brand new, sophisticated solutions to complex problems. People who collaborate and communicate freely, behave like leaders, adapt and change, and can operate from a place of deep mastery and learning—people who, above all else, recognize their infinite potential. You cannot have an unfear team or organization without unfear individuals. Later, we will describe how to create a context that helps other people step into their unfear selves.

Ultimately, though, we as humans can transform only one person—ourselves. So before you can succeed at an unfear transformation that permeates an entire organization, you must start with yourself.

The good news is that you already carry an unfear version of yourself. You just need to release it. This reminds us of what Michelangelo said when, in 1495, he finished "The Angel," an early masterwork: "I saw the angel in the marble and carved until I set him free." In much the same way, the unfear individual already exists within you. You just need to chisel away all the stone to set it free.

I (Gaurav) started my journey from fear to unfear at the age of 32. It was 2002, three years after I left Pepsi Cola to work as an associate in the marketing practice of McKinsey. The first dot-com bubble had just burst, and nobody was hiring marketing strategy consultants. One of my mentors suggested that I might find more opportunities in South Africa, so I requested a transfer to Johannesburg. On arrival, I realized that the office was in worse shape than the one in New York. The senior partners were looking for ways for the organization to rediscover its mojo. I'd been there for a few months when I received an email inviting all employees to attend a mindset workshop. I still remember rolling my eyes and thinking, "My career is going down the tube, and they're making me attend this shit."

At the time, I seemed like the paragon of a hard-charging, take-no-prisoners consultant: smart, articulate, hardworking, highly utilitarian. I, like several of my McKinsey colleagues, took pride in describing myself as an "insecure overachiever." I was in survival mode, displaying myriad fear archetypes. But I didn't perceive any of that as dysfunction—I just thought I was doing what I did best: fight, fight, and fight some more. Whenever something went wrong, I merely blamed someone else.

I was exactly the type of person to sneer at a mindset workshop. And that's exactly what I did on that warm November morning. I grumbled to any of my fellow participants who would listen what a waste of time the next two days would be. I had good reason for my skepticism. The firm had hired a 60-something British lady, who lived in Australia, to teach us about meditation. I took great pleasure in telling my cynical mates that Gita Bellin was a fraud, that she had chosen the name Gita to pretend to be a guru.[1]

I spent the entire first day of the workshop using my intellect to find fault with everything Gita said. The next morning, Gita led a meditation, and her soothing, monotonous voice broke through my defenses. I found myself relaxing and slipping beyond my thoughts to a place I had never been before. I lost all sense of space and time. As the meditation went on, I felt this energy rise within me. I felt like I was vibrating. I had never experienced anything like it before. After what seemed like an eternity, Gita led us out of the meditation and announced a break.

Everyone else went to the restroom or to have a smoke, but I was still vibrating, which concerned me. I didn't feel stable on my feet. I shared this with Gita. She calmly took me to a corner of the room and helped me get the vibration to subside. She asked me if I had ever had such an experience before, and I said no.

"What did you do to me?" I asked.

She smiled and told me that I had just felt a fraction of a vast untapped store of energy and insight that dwells in each human being. Hinduism calls it the *Kundalini*. Other wisdom traditions have different names for it, but to us, this is the angel within the stone—the beautiful, powerful being that lives within each of us that we can uncover and discover.

The rest of my day was a blissful daze. I smiled more than I ever had and felt that I had glimpsed a master key to life. The rational mind that had completely governed my life up to that moment was stunned into silence. Everything I thought I knew about the world and about my position in it was shattered. When my rational mind recovered (as it had to—I am the son of a physicist, after all), I felt that I needed to understand what had happened to me. I started studying with Gita, taking her workshops, meditating daily, and reading the ancient texts that she studied as well, all in an attempt to understand and explain the feeling and the transformation that had overcome me. I questioned how I perceived myself, life, and success. Even after all this work, I still can't explain what happened to me that day. But I know that it set me on a lifelong journey to carve away the stone so that I can free the angel within me.

This journey will never end, but I started noticing a change early on. I became a better husband, felt far happier, and performed better than I ever had before. I became friendlier and easier to work with, so much so that my supervisor at McKinsey started telling me to smile less so that clients would take me seriously. I started to understand, for the first time, what G. K. Chesterton meant when he said, "Angels can fly because they can take themselves lightly."

In this chapter, we will share some key lessons on how to unfear yourself to become a more effective leader, employee, and human being. From this place, you will be able to build unfear teams and unfear organizations. This initial step can be difficult and uncomfortable. It requires you to spend a lot of time in deep, honest reflection. There are no quick fixes or shortcuts. It is nothing short of fundamental: it creates the foundation for the rest of the unfear transformation.

You must start with transformational learning and then pair it with actions that will reinforce the transformation.

> *"Angels can fly because*
> *they can take themselves lightly."*
> —G. K. Chesterton[2]

Transformational Learning

There are two aspects of transformational learning that we need to unfear ourselves and unlock new levels of performance while enhancing personal well-being:

- Seeing the angel within: recognizing our infinite potential
- Clearing the unnecessary stone: operating from a place of mastery and learning

Seeing the Angel Within

This is the central claim of this entire book: we all carry within ourselves infinite potential—potential to do and to be anything. This might sound hokey, but it is actually an incredibly profound, powerful idea. That said, it is difficult to describe and define. Definitions, by their nature, are limiting, and anything that is truly infinite does not have limits. Yet it is a foundational idea because getting in touch with your infinite potential is the most important thing you can do to improve your performance and well-being. On the one hand, it allows us to be creative in our response to any life situation; on the other hand, it gives us access to an unlimited source of energy to embrace all the different facets of our lives with ease. Ultimately, what we are talking about when we refer to infinite potential is the nature of consciousness.

For thousands of years, philosophers and spiritualists, and more recently, psychologists, neuroscientists, and physicists, have tried to describe the nature of consciousness. With good reason. To understand consciousness is foundational to transformational learning. Knowledge of yourself and your consciousness is what allows you to use all the other knowledge you have most effectively because your state of being is the lens through which you see the world. It impacts how you view everything—how you view yourself, what you can accomplish, and what you think is possible. Understanding the inherent potential within consciousness allows you to transform yourself, to break through and alter whatever negative habits you have, so that you can live a joyful, creative life. It gives you a much greater degree of control to design your thoughts, feelings, beliefs, and ultimately, your life. Imagine yourself living from this place—vibrant, inexhaustible, creative, and joyful. Now imagine an organization full of such people.

This, we believe, is what Socrates meant when he said, "The unexamined life is not worth living."³ It's what the priests at the Temple of Delphi implored each visitor to do when they carved "Know Thyself" above the altar. It is what Carl Jung meant when he said, "Your visions will become clear only when you look into yourself. Who looks outside dreams, who looks inside awakens,"⁴ and what Buddha meant when he said, "Carpenters bend wood. Fletchers bend arrows. Wise men fashion themselves."⁵

> *Understanding the inherent potential within consciousness allows you to transform yourself, to break through and alter whatever negative habits you have, so that you can live a joyful, creative life.*

We must start with consciousness, which has infinite potential. It is limitless. To understand what we mean, it's best to start with a simple, concrete example of how we limit ourselves. In our work, we often meet executives who have taken personality assessments, such as DiSC, Myers-Briggs, or Discovery Insights. These executives then identify themselves with statements like "I am strong dominant," "I behave like this because I am an INTJ," and "That's because I am blue on Discovery Insights." With these statements, the executives unconsciously pigeonhole themselves. Even without personality tests, we do the same thing whenever we label ourselves with statements like "I am a procrastinator," "I am a conflict avoider," or "I am a perfectionist." Implicit in these statements is a limiting of our potential into how we've defined ourselves. This is even true of positive statements like "I am really good at problem solving" because implicit in this statement is a *but* about the other things you are not as good at.

Now all these statements have one thing in common: the word *I*. Everything else is only a qualifier of the I. When we talk about infinite

potential, our angel, our invitation is for you to reflect on the unconditioned and unlimited I.

To spur this reflection, ask yourself two questions. First, ask: do I have
any thoughts or ideas inside my head at this very moment? The answer,
almost always, is yes. Then ask: how do I know I have those ideas or
thoughts? With enough reflection, you'll realize that there are two parts of
you operating at the same time—one part we call the *actor*, who is thinking, and the other part we call the *observer*, who is observing the thinking.

When we identify with just the actor, we define ourselves according
to how we are acting or behaving in a given moment. Whenever we fall
into the fear archetypes, we are only identifying with the actor. All those
stories we tell ourselves—"I have to control my employees so that they
work," "I have to spend hours on this or it won't be perfect"—put limits
on ourselves and our behavior.

This isn't to say that identifying as the actor is bad. In fact, it is essential. The actor is the instrument through which we express ourselves.
However, to really unlock our potential, we must remember that we are
also the observer. When we do this, we gain access to a whole new capacity. We realize that even as we act, we can observe ourselves acting. Put
another way, we realize that we are not our thoughts, ideas, and emotions,
but rather we *have* our thoughts, ideas and emotions. And because we
have thoughts, ideas, and emotions, we have the power of choice that
allows us to orchestrate the future rather than live at the mercy of the past.

From this understanding, we learn that we can shift any of those
thoughts, ideas, and emotions whenever we want to or need to. In other
words, we can change the type of actor that we are. We no longer say,
"I'm a perfectionist; therefore, I have to spend x number of hours on this
project." Instead, we can notice our tendency toward perfectionism and
then move ourselves closer to actual effectiveness and make sure that we
get things done. This understanding of ourselves allows us to be adaptive
and resilient in the face of any situation.

This orientation also shifts our relationship with fear. Fear becomes
one of the many emotions we experience as the actor and something we

have choice over as the observer. When we feel fear, we don't have to collapse into a fear archetype—a comfortable, habitual, and reactive pattern. Instead, we can choose to step into one of the unfear archetypes and use it to guide our learning and growth. This orientation and ability have obvious benefits in the business world.

> *Fear becomes one of the many emotions*
> *we experience as the actor and something*
> *we have choice over as the observer.*

For example, the pandemic gave us at Co-Creation Partners a great opportunity to practice stepping into the unfear archetypes. Prior to Covid-19, we conducted almost all our work face-to-face (and swore up and down to anyone who would listen that we could never do our client work effectively in a remote environment). As soon as the pandemic hit, our entire client pipeline dried up. Our clients, and frankly ourselves, couldn't see a way to continue our work safely. We easily could have slipped into a reactive pattern and cut our expenses, let go of team members, and just hoped that the pandemic would end. Instead, we spent about a week bemoaning our plight (even we, sometimes, feel helpless), but eventually we stepped into our observer mode and took ownership of our future. Within a month, we taught ourselves the ways of the virtual world and developed a minimum viable product. Over the next month, we tested it internally and eventually rolled it out. Our clients were thrilled and impressed by what we could do digitally, and several of them adopted some of our virtual practices. The point is that in the face of fear, when we channel the observer, we can choose our response. We can step into resilience and creativity, or we can stay stuck in fear, negativity, and self-pity.

A key part of recognizing your infinite potential requires you to recognize the infinite potential of everyone else. You cannot realize that your consciousness is limitless and then try to control everyone else and bend them to your will. Doing so would run counter to the idea of infinite potential. You'd be falling into the Aggressive/Defensive archetype. Historically, this is the ego-based stance some senior leaders have when running organizations—as if they are magically bestowed with infinite potential while everyone else is not. Such a belief comes from fear and a need to control others and is deeply dysfunctional. Such a stance prevents organizations from accessing the incredible creativity and ability latent in their employees. As Dwight Eisenhower said, "You do not lead people by hitting them over the head—that's assault, not leadership."[6]

> *Recognizing your infinite potential requires you to recognize the infinite potential of everyone else.*

Let us close this section with a little anecdote, which is both silly and deep at the same time. A minicrisis once broke out in the Bhatnagar household. My (Gaurav's) daughter needed to email her homework to a teacher, but the internet wasn't working. She was home with my wife, Shobha, and they both started to freak out. Shobha called Cablevision for customer support. The service rep insisted that the Wi-Fi was working, but nobody could connect. Eventually, when the rep instructed Shobha to restart the router, she saw that it had been accidentally unplugged. The Wi-Fi was not connected to its power source.

Our belief in our own infinite potential is our energy source. When we disconnect from our source (or, more accurately, are weakly connected to it), we feel depleted and cannot sustain our intention to operate from the four unfear archetypes.

> *Our belief in our own infinite potential is our energy source.*

Clearing the Unnecessary Stone

The second aspect of transformational learning that we need to unlock performance and well-being requires us to shift two mindsets:

- From victim to mastery
- From knower to learner

Transforming these mindsets is fundamental to spurring individual learning—to prioritizing growth in how we are *being* and in what we are *doing*.

From Victim to Mastery

To demonstrate the victim mindset, we do a simple exercise with our clients. We hold up a pen and then let it go. When we ask, "Why did the pen fall?," most people respond, "Gravity."

We then promise to do some magic that will make gravity disappear. With much theatrics, we hold up the pen again. This time we don't drop it. The pen (obviously) doesn't fall, and we ask, "Why didn't the pen fall?"

People answer, "Because you did not let it go."

We push back and say that if the pen fell because of gravity, then we must have made gravity disappear.

The way that most people respond to the first question is representative of the victim mindset. They claim that something negative (the pen falling) happened because of an external force (gravity) rather than because of a choice that we made (to let go). When we operate in the victim mindset, we believe that we are at the mercy of our circumstances. In the victim mindset, we believe ourselves powerless against some big, bad *they* (e.g., management, another department, direct reports, shareholders, customers, etc.) that has profound control over us. We always blame someone or something else when things go wrong. This is one of the mindsets that hardens like marble, imprisoning the angel within.

Even though this mindset blocks us from our source of energy, it can be very difficult to escape. It offers our egos (the way that we view ourselves) a false sense of security—we can continue to believe that we are exceptionally talented/creative/hardworking even in the face of failure if we blame all those failures on something other than ourselves. We can also weaponize this mindset to garner sympathy. We use the victim mindset to absolve ourselves of any responsibility for our emotions and actions. It makes us feel innocent, even when we are in the wrong or have made a mistake.

Yet, when we eschew responsibility, we disempower ourselves. Just think about the word *responsible* and its component parts: *response* and *able*. When you deny responsibility, you deny your *ability* to *respond* to your situation. You give up your power and hand it over to other people, which leaves you trapped in a web of reaction.

We acquire this mindset at a very young age. When a child spills milk, he usually says, "It fell," not "I dropped it." When the child becomes an adult and arrives late for an early-morning meeting, he says that the traffic was bad. In this case, the bad traffic, like gravity, exists. But when the adult points to it as the reason for being late, he also fails to mention that he didn't plan for it properly. If you listen carefully, you will hear victim statements everywhere in your organization.

> *When you deny responsibility, you deny your ability to respond to your situation. You give up your power and hand it over to other people.*

The first step to building a high-performing organization is to encourage people to shift from this victim mindset to a mindset of mastery. The mastery mindset is perhaps best articulated by Austrian neurologist, psychiatrist, and Holocaust survivor Viktor Frankl in his memoir, *Man's Search for Meaning.*[7]

We who lived in concentration camps can remember the men who walked through the huts comforting others, giving away their last piece of bread. They may have been few in number, but they offer sufficient proof that everything can be taken from a man but one thing: the last of the human freedoms—to choose one's attitude in any given set of circumstances, to choose one's own way.

Frankl describes the central idea of the mastery mindset, the awareness that while we might not control our circumstances, we always have a choice about how we respond.

There are six core beliefs we need to hold to live in a mastery mindset:

1. Mastery means not blaming ourselves. We must not victimize ourselves. Instead, we should reframe the internal dialogue to "I did the best I could given the person I was." This creates more space for us to step into a different version of ourselves.

2. Mastery means being aware of the multitude of choices available to us in any given situation.

3. Mastery means being aware of when and where we are not taking responsibility so that we can eventually transform. Anger, excuses, deflections, and fear are great clues that indicate when we are not taking responsibility.

4. Mastery requires us to become aware of the payoffs that keep us stuck in our current situation and patterns.

5. When we are in mastery, we look for the opportunities and upsides in challenges, not just the dangers or annoyances. We view the most challenging people in our lives as great gifts that allow us to express our potential in new and different ways. As Carl Jung said, "Everything that irritates us about others can lead us to an understanding of ourselves."[8]

6. Mastery means being bold enough to know and declare what we want in life and act on it.

Creating a mindset of mastery helps individuals see challenging situations as learning opportunities that they can get through instead of as a threat to avoid. Just as oysters create pearls from the irritants that slip between their shells, we can embrace challenges as opportunities for growth and convert our infinite potential into performance. The irritants are necessary conditions—not something to avoid.

> *The central idea of the mastery mindset is the awareness that while we might not control our circumstances, we always have a choice about how we respond.*

Let us look at the pandemic as an example. Historically, it takes many years to develop a vaccine. At the start of the pandemic, several doomsday prognosticators insisted that it would take years to develop a vaccine and that any vaccine would be 50 percent effective at best. It would have been easy for governments and pharmaceutical companies to fall into the victim mindset and just assume that accelerated vaccine development would not be possible. Instead, multiple governments and organizations saw it as a challenge, an opportunity to discover a way to expedite a lengthy process safely. They did several things with little to no precedent, including a tremendous degree of worldwide collaboration and data sharing. They also used, for the first time outside of clinical trials, messenger RNA (mRNA) technology. This technology, essentially, allowed them to create a vaccine that replicates parts of the virus's protein instead of having to breed weakened versions of the pathogen, as is done in traditional vaccine processes. The crisis prompted all these institutions to create new steps, to learn to work in new ways and with new technologies. They achieved an unprecedented result, delivering multiple vaccines in fewer than 12 months, all with exceptionally high efficacy.[9]

A quick caveat: we aren't saying that negative, unfair things don't happen. They can and do. Neither do we absolve systems or individuals of oppressive, offensive, and violent acts. The mindset shift we invite you to consider is about connecting to your agency and your power in the face of those circumstances.

From Knower to Learner

In the knower mindset, we act as if our beliefs and stories are the immutable truth. This mindset impacts our opinions on everything from economic policy and company strategy down to whether a given meeting will be a waste of time. As the knower, we believe that the past is a perfect predictor of the future. If the last meeting with someone was a waste of time, we know that the next meeting also will be. Our internal dialogue generates our future, so if we believe that, then we show up to the meeting grumpy and closed off, and the meeting is definitely a waste of time. In this sense, with this mindset, we allow the past to become a thief that steals our present and future. It prevents us from seeing the possibilities in new ideas or situations because we let the past negatively color our opinions.

In contrast, in the learner mindset, we recognize that we do not know everything about the world. We hold our opinions more lightly, we believe that everyone and every situation can teach us something new, and perhaps most important, we acknowledge that everything is ever evolving and that every moment is ripe with possibility, no matter what happened in the past. This isn't to say that we ignore the past. Instead, we draw from our past knowledge and use it to impact our choices, recognizing that we might be surprised.

To return to the meeting example, with a learner mindset, we might go to the second meeting looking for ways to better engage with our colleague. The learner mindset reinforces the mastery mindset because it holds that we are not at the mercy of circumstances and the past. We can change, and each situation can evolve in ways that we would never expect.

In the same way, the knower mindset reinforces the victim mentality. Let's say someone comes up with a new idea to improve team dynamics.

The boss instantly shuts it down, and that employee never shares a new idea. The internal tape of the victim mindset says, "My boss is unreasonable, so I better keep quiet," and the internal tape of the knower mindset adds, "My boss will never change and will never seriously consider my opinion." By controlling our internal narrative, the victim and knower mindsets also keep us trapped in the fear archetypes. In this example, the mindsets reinforce the Minion archetype, a person who believes that she can never challenge her boss; she just needs to keep her head down and stay in line.

The more we experience such situations, the more tempting it can be to sink into a knower mindset. This is why without a careful, proactive effort to stay in the learner mindset, most people sink further into a knower orientation the longer they stay at a company. The more accustomed to the established processes of an organization people get, the more they believe that to be the only way to do things, and innovation plummets. This is why in most organizations the majority of new ideas come from new people. When employees embrace a learner mindset, organizations don't have to rely on bringing in fresh talent to come up with innovative ideas. The talent's often there all along; it's just obscured by certain mindsets.

Likewise, a learner mindset helps leaders develop better strategies and take more calculated risks. Leaders with the knower mindset refuse to listen to new ideas while they doggedly maintain past strategies, even when they fail to produce the desired results. In contrast, leaders with the learner mindset see the possibilities posed by new ways of doing things and are willing to experiment.

A leader stuck in a knower mindset also impacts employee development and turnover. Leaders with this mindset see their employees as fixed entities with a limited capacity to learn and grow, so instead of taking the time to coach and develop them, they just replace them. But the business landscape is in constant flux. Hiring for new ideas is an extremely expensive and disruptive way to innovate and grow.

A knower mindset also negatively impacts conversations about diversity, equity, and inclusion. Knowers have preconceived and fixed notions about the capabilities and intentions of other groups based on the conditioning they've received in their lives. They often hold these as incontrovertible truths which subconsciously and consciously shape their behaviors.

During my (Gaurav's) time in South Africa, I became very friendly with someone whose father was a senior official in the apartheid government. I felt close enough to him to ask him why whites behaved the way they did toward the native, Asian, and people of color in the country. I will never forget his response.

> *We need to allow our assumptions to be challenged and changed without shame or blame.*

He told me that from a very young age he was taught that whites were superior to other races, and therefore, it was their job to protect and teach the other races. Fortunately, my friend had a learner mindset and was open to experiences that would challenge or alter those racial beliefs. As a teen, he took a long train trip through Africa, always sitting in the cheap seats. He met strangers of different races. He had the long, candid, honest, and reflective conversations that one does when one is stuck in close quarters with strangers for significant periods of time. He learned that the stories he had been told growing up did not make any sense. This man now has a tremendous ability to connect with other humans, to see them for who they are, and to engage in productive, respectful conversations. But he also told me that some of the people he grew up with were stuck in the knower mindset and couldn't see past their racist conditioning. This is an extreme example, but the core point is that to build a diverse, equitable, and inclusive organization, we need to enter conversations with an open mind. We need to be willing to surface and be honest about our conditioned assumptions about race, gender, sexual orientation, socioeconomic status, level of education, or any other markers of identity. Then we need to allow our assumptions to be challenged and changed without shame or blame. In short, we need to attempt to understand the other person's point of view.

Embracing the learner mindset is a lifelong practice, and most of us will flit between the learner and knower mindsets sometimes even in the same day. There are six simple daily practices to help us get into and stay in the learner mindset:

1. Take ownership over our thoughts, feelings, and assumptions with "I" statements (e.g., "I think that we should . . .") instead of presenting your beliefs as common fact with statements such as, "Everyone knows that we should . . .".

2. Demonstrate humility and curiosity when presented with an alternative perspective, even when we are the expert in the subject matter. This creates space for a new mix of ideas and perspectives to emerge.

3. Look forward rather than backward. Don't dwell too much on why something went wrong. Instead, recognize the value in reflection and diagnostics, but keep most of your focus on solutions and the future.

4. Stay away from the language of absolutes. *Always* and *never* are rarely accurate terms and can reflect a knower mindset.

5. Prioritize being effective over being right. Doing this allows us to combine our wisdom and expertise with those of other people and find a solution that works best for each stakeholder instead of just ourselves.

6. Be just as curious about what we do *not* know as about what we do know (or think we do).

Action Learning

To become an unfear individual, it's not enough to simply decide to change our mindsets. To unfear takes practice. It requires actions, and those actions are the tools we use to chisel away the excess marble trapping the angel. All these tools are just different ways to apply the two human superpowers—language and imagination—to reframe our relationship with fear. They are a series of conversations that we have with ourselves or that we notice having with ourselves.

These habits and practices of the mind are fundamental to performance and well-being. Unfortunately, most people pay far less attention to these intrapersonal skills than they do to technical and interpersonal skills. Most organizations place more weight on "objective" knowledge and capabilities. Although this knowledge helps us manage and improve our operations, the quality of our thoughts ultimately drives the quality of our life, relationships, and work. Learning how to manage those thoughts and emotions helps us apply our technical skills, see the business landscape with clarity, and respond with creativity. It helps us show up without limits and remain balanced in the face of pressure. The three essential unfear practices are mindfulness, authentic humility, and examining our core values.

Unfear Practice 1: Mindfulness

We can break down mindfulness into two practices: self-awareness and self-regulation. Together they allow us to access self-knowledge, which is the key to leveraging and understanding all other knowledge. They also enable us to recognize when our mindset does not aid us in the task at hand (awareness) and to consciously alter it (regulation). Mindfulness offers a plethora of advantages in life. It can help us live more fully and more peacefully in every domain, improve our relationships, reduce stress, bolster mental and physical health, and find a sense of balance and purpose.

People often assume that everyone is either born with the ability to be self-aware and to self-regulate or they aren't. The truth is that self-awareness and self-regulation are skills that we can learn and improve throughout life. They are muscles that you can build at any point in your day-to-day life. For example, when you're in a meeting, you may notice the interplay of your emotions with your thoughts and your bodily sensations and how that pulls you to act in a certain way. With this awareness, you could choose to respond differently. This combines awareness and regulation. It moves you from being at the mercy of your circumstances to a place of choice. You can intervene in more creative ways to be effective in any given situation. The power of mindfulness is that it allows you to be aware of how your mind is operating so that you can choose to act rather than react.

One way to practice this is meditation. In its simplest form, meditation is just an invitation to observe and consciously choose. Observe your breath, your thoughts, your emotions. When your observation strays from your breath to your thoughts, consciously choose to focus once more on your breath. Through this simple practice, we strengthen our ability to remember that we are both the actor—the one breathing, thinking, and feeling—and the observer—the one noticing. As the observer, we have the choice to consciously move from our thoughts to our breath or vice versa. As we continue meditating, the observer becomes more powerful. We deepen our ability to perceive ourselves, our state, and our surroundings. Instead of identifying as the actor and getting caught in the emotional peaks and valleys of everyday life, we learn how to view ourselves and everything around us at once. It is like looking down from a balcony at a performance that we are also in, seeing how everything flows together, and adjusting our actions so that we are much more in concert with our surroundings.

While we strongly recommend having a formal meditation practice, it is not the only way to achieve mindfulness. Repetitive exercises such as running allow us to slip into a meditative state and observe our thoughts, as does walking (especially through nature), prayer, and reading books while paying a deep degree of attention to the content. The goal is to have both the observer and actor perspectives accessible in every part of your life.

> *Ultimately, all mindfulness practices are a means to an end. The end is to be mindful, to have both observer and actor perspectives available simultaneously in every moment of our daily lives.*

Mindfulness has three key benefits in a business context:

1. **It allows us to regulate our emotions.** When we feel fear arise, poised to sabotage us and throw us into dysfunctional patterns, the self-awareness and regulation gained from practicing mindfulness enables us to consciously structure our thoughts in a productive way. This prevents us from being thrown off balance too often, from being hijacked by the amygdala. If we find ourselves being reactive, we can press "Pause," reconnect with the observer, let the stress hormones leave our body, and recognize the diversity of choices available to us. We can access new perspectives and choose how to respond to be effective in the moment. Although each situation is different, there are two important questions to ask in the face of any challenge: What other choices can I make right now? and What can I learn here?

   The more we practice this awareness, the more we discover that emotions are incredibly short lived. An amygdala hijack takes a fraction of a second, and the emotional fallout dissipates within seconds or minutes of the threat disappearing. We only perceive emotions as long lasting when we ruminate on an issue, which continually retriggers the emotional response. Through practice, however, we can recognize the trigger–response cycle and consciously choose to stop ruminating, moving us away from emotional reactivity and giving us the opportunity to see new possibilities for action. This practice is crucial to living in the mindset of mastery.

> *What other choices can I make right now? What can I learn here?*

2. **Mindfulness helps us recognize our mindset and how it shapes our perspective and approach to business problems.** When we say mindset, we mean any belief we have that colors how we interpret the world. This includes our beliefs about values, justice, politics, economics, and religion—these all contribute to how we make decisions. More often than not, we are blind to our own mindsets. This can have devastating consequences because our mindsets limit the strategic options that we see. According to Peter Senge, a senior lecturer at the MIT Sloan School of Business, debates about strategy matter less than debates about the mindsets that drive that strategy. For example, we interviewed the head of strategy for a leading consumer goods company. She told us that the challenge with driving growth in her company didn't come from a lack of new ideas. Rather, it came from the resistance she faced from senior leaders. They were all fixed in their mindsets, believing that the only way forward was the one they'd always known and done. These mindsets were driven and sustained by fear: the senior leaders were afraid that if the company moved in a new direction, then it would no longer need their knowledge and talents, and they would lose their positions. With better awareness of these beliefs, the leadership team may have made much more effective decisions.

Through practice, we develop the ability to step on a balcony and observe our mindsets and assumptions about how the world works. We can ask ourselves how we think the world operates and then see if we latch onto bits of information that confirm our assumptions. Almost all of us do this, but now when we realize that we seek confirmation of our beliefs, we can look for information that makes us uncomfortable, that challenges those beliefs and assumptions. Those places of discomfort are usually places of learning and growth. This will ultimately improve strategic agility and decision-making capabilities. This practice is crucial to living the mindset of a learner.

> *Places of discomfort are usually*
> *places of learning and growth.*

3. **We can train our mind, at will, to access different brain wave patterns.** This can be a huge driver of performance. Different activities, from linear thinking to empathy, require access to different brain waves, and practicing mindfulness—meditation in particular—allows you to tune into them and then shift between them. To do this, close your eyes for 30 seconds. This enables you to shift your focus from your external world to your internal world and eliminates a lot of sensory stimuli. This will immediately reduce your metabolic rate. Then open your eyes just a little and then close your eyes again. Then, very gently, begin to be aware of the rise and fall of your breath. As you have thoughts, just notice them and let them pass, and go back to your breath. You will find yourself settling into your breath and your breath becoming slower and finer. As this happens, you start moving from beta to alpha to theta to delta (more on these in a bit).

   Meditation is like exercise—the more you do it, the better you get. As you practice shifting your brain waves using this method, you will gain the ability to access different brain waves even when you're not in a calm environment. You can be in the chaos of a meeting, and all you need to do is center yourself with your breathing, and you will be able to find the brain wave state most needed in the moment.

Brain waves are measured in cycles per second (cps) and are divided into four main categories.[10] The descriptions that follow are broad oversimplifications. In practice, the brain and the electronic pulses it creates are far more complex, but this basic understanding illustrates how powerful it can be to gain the ability to consciously access and transition between different brain waves:

1. **Beta brain waves** have the highest frequency at about 14–38 cps. If we were connected to an electroencephalograph (EEG), this would be the predominant brain wave that would show up on our graph. Beta brain waves are best for logical, linear thinking and multitasking. They are also the brain waves most associated with stress. For a sense of what being in beta feels like, imagine a busy day spent running from meeting to meeting, struggling to keep several balls in the air, only to get home exhausted and collapse into bed. Then imagine not being able to fall asleep because your brain won't shut down. Even if you do sleep, you wake up the next day exhausted.

2. **Alpha brain waves** have a frequency of 8–14 cps. These brain waves are associated with single-pointed focus and help us get things accomplished in a very effective manner. For a sense of what this experience feels like, imagine getting so lost in work that you lose track of time and space, and suddenly you're 30 minutes late for a meeting. Or you're reading a great book, and the next thing you know, it has been three hours.

3. **Theta brain waves** have a frequency of 4–8 cps. They are associated with nonlinear thinking, creativity, and memory. To know what this feels like, think about when you're at your most creative. Usually we feel most creative early in the morning or while we're taking a shower, running, or relaxing. This is because all these activities slow your brain waves down, either because you're focusing on some other habitual/repetitive task (e.g., running, showering) or because you're in a laid-back, near-sleep state (e.g., mornings, relaxing). Memory also lives in theta. Have you ever come across someone at an office party, recognized their face, but could not remember their name? You tried as hard as you could

to remember, to no avail. Then, later that night, while you're relaxing at home, you suddenly remember the name. That's because you've sunk from beta down to theta, where memories start to surface.

4. **Delta brain waves** run from 0.5–4 cps. They are most associated with intuition and empathetic radar. You are usually in delta when you know, in your gut, that you should do something, even when the data disagree. This, like theta, can occur during waking hours, but is far more common when we are asleep.

If most of us hard-charging executive types spent the entire day hooked to an EEG machine, it would show almost exclusively beta brain waves. This can be good—executives are busy, have to multitask, and need to be able to make logical decisions. However, we also need to be able to tap into the alpha and theta states to focus on a single issue for a long time and to make bold, creative strategic decisions.

Meditation provides us with the capacity to consciously move from one brain wave to another. The more you practice intentionally moving from beta to alpha and theta, the easier it gets. It's like developing a muscle. After meditating consistently, you develop the ability to move into whatever brain wave pattern is best suited to whatever work you need to accomplish.

In our workshops, we use this knowledge of brain waves to create different moods to trigger breakthroughs. For example, if we're working with a team in high beta that's struggling to come up with new ideas, we try to lead them into an alpha-theta state. We might invite them to a nature workshop (perhaps an activity such as a hike). Conversation slows, allowing creative ideas to flow. Similarly, when teams struggle with trust and connection, we do late-evening reflective exercises that allow participants to access delta. From there, they open up parts of themselves that they would not normally reveal during the day or in "professional" settings.

Unfear Practice 2: Authentic Humility

A great way to step into the learner mindset is to practice authentic humility. The authenticity part is important. People can easily detect false humility, and if you are merely saying self-deprecating things while ignoring everyone else's input, you will remain in a knower mindset. Authentic humility can only come from confidence. To be humble, you must first acknowledge your skills, accomplishments, and expertise. You need to be able to trust yourself to execute and to make the right decisions in difficult circumstances—but you also understand that you alone will never have all the answers. In a somewhat paradoxical way, true confidence requires true humility. You can only know that you are making the right decision in a business environment when you're able to see outside yourself. There are three steps to practicing authentic humility:

1. **Master the language of "I don't know" with regard to future outcomes.** We aren't saying that you should pretend that you have no experience or knowledge. Rather, this is about being conscious of the ways that your internal conversations either prepare you for or prevent you from learning. Using statements like "I'm not sure, but my hypothesis is . . ." or "I wonder what . . . they think about this/will happen when we/the data say about this aspect . . ." instead of the language of certainty, "I know this will happen . . . ," will enable you to keep an open mind and seek out more information as you make decisions. Be curious.

2. **Acquire context and the ability to see nuances.** Context allows us to see what others don't or what we couldn't before we acquired that context. For example, imagine someone who has never heard of golf strolling through a golf course. She would see long stretches of grass, winding paths, pools of water, patches of sand, and people with sticks hitting balls. Imagine that the person runs into Mark, an avid golfer, who explains the differences between the fairway, the rough, and the greens; the sand and water hazards; the tee box; and

the different clubs you use depending on the shot you're trying to make. The next time this person strolls through the golf course, she will see it differently. She sees golfers hitting from the rough and notices the different cuts of grass on the various parts of the course. She missed all this the first time because she didn't have the context to process what she was seeing. After understanding the context, this person could see what had been previously invisible to her unconditioned eyes.

Now imagine if Mark attended a putting clinic by Phil Mickelson, a golf great who has won more than 40 events on the PGA Tour, and Phil asked Mark to describe the green. Mark would describe the slope of the green, how even or uneven the surface is, and the level of dew on the grass. Now Phil asks which direction the grass has been cut and whether Mark is putting with or against the cut. Suddenly Mark sees the green with fresh eyes. Mark can only achieve this new level of awareness, however, if he approaches the putting clinic with humility and a willingness to learn. If he came with the goal of showing off to Mickelson, he would likely get too caught up in his ego to really listen to and internalize Phil's teaching.

This example highlights a key fact: we see through our eyes, but we observe and understand through our ability to see the subtle nuances revealed by context. To live in a learner's mindset is to continue to deepen and diversify our ability to understand context. Doing so will make new possibilities visible to you, in any part of life, including business. For example, imagine a lifelong operations expert who becomes a CEO. This person has deep expertise in operations and will view each part of the organization through that lens. But what if the organization faces challenges in marketing and growth? In technological security? In workplace culture? To be successful, the CEO needs to diversify her ability to acquire context and then deepen them in each new field instead of just applying operational solutions to every problem.

Through this process, you can begin to combine diverse perspectives to find new, surprising solutions to problems. It enables us to see that different is just different, not right or wrong. It allows us to be inclusive of others, to not break down into the classic divides of function and silo, and to embrace diversity of thought as a key asset within the organization as it faces ever-increasing and changing business challenges.

3. **Focus on the process, not merely the outcomes.** We aren't saying that outcomes don't matter—they obviously do, and they can mean the difference between your business succeeding and failing. That said, we can't fully control outcomes because they rely on too many variables. When people tie their sense of self-worth to outcomes, it leads to a brittle self-confidence. They beat themselves up when they come up short and fall into all sorts of negative, fear-based patterns. Because of this, they never engage in an in-depth examination of what led to the outcomes they are experiencing, so they never actually learn what truly happened and why they might have fallen short. And because they don't learn, then they make no changes to their behavior.

The practice of authentic humility is critical to engaging in conversations related to diversity, equity, and inclusion. When we approach this topic with authentic humility, we acknowledge that we do not know the other's perspective. This creates curiosity about the context people of different ethnicities, genders, and sexual orientations experience. We can enter into these conversations with a desire to understand, as opposed to a desire to impose our view as the universal truth. This creates a space for open dialogue rather than people talking past each other.

Unfear Practice 3: Examining Our Core Values

"Live your values!" We hear this all the time. Although living a purposeful and values-driven life is an admirable goal, many of us have a far too shallow understanding of what it means to live your values. The challenge is that most people don't just identify their values—they identify *with* their values.

When we become too identified with our values, we slip into self-righteousness and dysfunction. We see others as wrong for seemingly not sharing the values that we hold dear. We negatively judge people who have different values than us. We cling so hard to our values that we don't allow them to be challenged. In other words, we close ourselves off to dialogue and learning. We reinforce a knower mindset.

Each fear archetype presents a great example of this because each of these archetypes holds certain values strongly. Controllers and Minions value stability, Likables value friendship and belonging, and Perfectionists value achievement and high quality. In a vacuum, all these values are important. Problems arise—the dysfunctions we identified in Chapter 3—when we interpret threats to these values as threats to ourselves and fall back on fear-based behaviors.

We can, however, use our values to better understand and guide our actions and to serve as a bridge that will connect us with others. There are two skills that allow us to leverage our values in a productive way:

1. **Notice our values and hold them lightly.** Rather than immutable, unquestionable expressions of "who we are," values, like our thoughts, emotions, and beliefs, are things that we have. And if you pay careful attention, over time, in your life, they sometimes change. From the standpoint of the observer, our values can be noticed. And if you can notice something, you're not stuck being that thing. When we realize this, we can have our values, but we can hold them more lightly. We can choose how we want to express and act on them. We can approach our values with openness and awareness rather than defensiveness and mindlessness.

    For example, we once coached an executive in a financial services company with a strong Likable tendency. This leader struggled with coaching and providing feedback to an underperforming team member because he was afraid that it would lead to hurt feelings and resentment and introduce negativity to his team. In our conversations, this leader reflected on the value he placed on harmony and team cohesion. He learned to investigate whether the values, as he was holding them, were serving him and his team. He realized that they weren't. As he explored his values, he realized that he had other, more important values to express. He wanted his team member to grow and succeed, and he cared more about that than about being liked. This self-exploration of values then made it easier for this leader to articulate to this employee what was important to him: "I value your growth and development and success on the team." From there he was able to deliver the tough feedback in a positive way that not only sparked and inspired the employee to perform but also contributed to team cohesion.

This is what happens when we explore our own values. We see where different values are in tension. Rather than clinging hard to one or the other, we can notice these tensions and allow that to guide us to new creative actions.

2. **Explore our values more deeply.** The deeper we probe, the greater is the overlap we find between our values and those of others. A good example of this can be found in any political debate that breaks out at family gatherings. The debaters spout off about their values to prove everyone else's waywardness: "voting rights!," "voting integrity!," "justice!," "compassion!," "liberalism!," "conservatism!," "peace!," "defense!," "collusion!," "no collusion!"

All these terms are loaded with meaning, but they're all expressions of personal values. The more we reflect on the actual underlying desire that motivates these values, the more overlap we find between seemingly contradictory ideas. For instance, reflecting on the "voting rights" and "voting integrity" terms, one may realize that beyond these are values such as "equal opportunity under the law," "one person, one vote," "fair representation," "democracy," and so on. For most values we hold, there are almost always deeper, more expansive or inclusive levels to them. We may disagree on how a value can be achieved, but we may discover that our deeper values overlap more than we think.

These two realizations and practices will help us lead more value-driven and purposeful lives in a way that connects us more deeply with others. They will help us learn from people who see the world differently than we do and create collective action toward shared goals. They will, in short, help us learn to become effective members of unfear teams.

WORTH THINKING ABOUT

- How does your belief about your own potential enable or limit you? What limiting stories about yourself or others might you be stuck in?

- How might you be showing up with a victim or knower mindset in your life? How does this impact your effectiveness?

- Are you aware of your thoughts or emotional patterns at any given moment? What additional choices would be available if you had this awareness?

- What practices can you employ to improve your capacity for personal mastery, self-awareness, and self-regulation?

6

The Unfear Team
Building the Jazz Ensemble

J
azz—a true American art form, an amalgamation, a blending of the musical traditions of immigrants and enslaved people who came to these shores. Jazz is beautiful, complex, and completely unique. And you can't quite define it, but you always know it when you hear it. As Louis Armstrong is reported to have said when asked, what is jazz? "If you have to ask, you will never know."

A jazz ensemble—woodwinds, percussion, strings, and vocals—is no different from a team with its many personalities. When an ensemble is on, really and truly on, it is magic—it creates music that touches the soul. It blends the personal styles of each player to create beautiful, unique combinations. It transforms both the performers and the audience, and it transports everyone to the realm of the sublime. But when it's off, it is a disaster of epic proportions. The same is true of a team within an organization—when it is gelling, it can deliver outcomes far greater than the sum of its parts. And it does so with joy and creativity, no matter how difficult the task, building affinity within the team and making others want to be part of it.

Jazz ensembles and high-performing teams both rely on improvisation, on staying in the present moment with one another. On the best teams, each member is able to bounce ideas off the others and pick up a new thought and run with it. Team members are constantly inviting and combining perspectives, integrating the unique ideas of each other to create something new and beautiful.

Improvisation and staying in the present moment often instill fear. We feel fear when we aren't certain about what will happen and when we force ourselves to stay present and confront uncomfortable situations. On teams, improvising and staying in the present instill even more fear because we rely on everyone else to also perform. We can't perform to the best of our abilities if we are constantly worrying about everyone else, and we can't improvise and stay in the present if we don't believe that others will honor our vulnerability, listen to us, and build on our ideas. Everyone needs to relinquish control, to live in collective uncertainty, to flow, and to improvise. The key to unlocking all of this is trust. Trust is the bridge between the individual and the team. To become a highly effective team, you have to trust that, collectively, you can create outcomes far greater than any individual can.

In this chapter, we will share the mindset shifts and practices that we have seen help individuals work more effectively on teams. Use these tools to unfear your own team. Even if you are not the formal leader of your team, you can still influence others and spark a transformation. In fact, the skills and mindsets we lay out here will help you have the conversations necessary to bring about this transformation. They will enable you to build your own sublime jazz ensemble.

Transformational Learning

We see two critical mindset shifts that are needed to create the foundation for building high-performing teams. These mindsets are fundamental to building trust, encouraging candor, and drawing the best from each team member. These shifts are from right/wrong to effectiveness and from label to label to human to human.

From Right/Wrong to Effectiveness

In the right/wrong mindset, we believe that our solution to a given problem is the only correct one. This mindset springs from a biological urge. According to the neurologist Robert Burton, feeling certain activates the same neurologic reward circuits as sex and gambling.[1] Most of our early life reinforces this affinity. Being right helps us score well on tests, receive good grades, get into college, and eventually land a job. By the time most people reach adulthood, they're firmly entrenched in a right/wrong mindset.

The problem is that once we move out of the world of standardized tests, it becomes impossible to always be right. In the real world, most problems have myriad solutions, and most disagreements stem from different perspectives. There is no right answer or right interpretation of an event, but our stubborn belief that our solution is the only solution often causes dysfunction within a team. When we view the world this way, we lose the ability to compromise, to find solutions that work for every stakeholder, and to combine different ideas and perspectives to create something new.

The unfear mindset is one of effectiveness. When we live in the effectiveness mindset, the question we ask ourselves isn't, "How can I prove to everyone that I'm right?" Instead, we ask, "How can I create effective movement toward a solution to this problem?" This framing encourages us to hold our interpretations and solutions lightly and to open ourselves up to new ideas. This mindset shift leads to two transformative outcomes: moving from self-righteousness to curiosity and encouraging creativity and ownership.

From Self-Righteousness to Curiosity

In late 2020, we joined a colleague from another consulting firm to work on a large-scale transformation program for an international travel and logistics company. One of the major sources of friction in this company came from the relationship between the head of their US operations—a brilliant, high-performing man named Olivier—and the CEO and other executives based in the European headquarters. Olivier had turned around the French division of the company, and headquarters had sent him to the failing US arm, hoping that he could do the same.

He had similar success in the United States, yet his peers struggled to work with him. Olivier is a tremendous salesperson because he can diagnose and solve a customer's problem better than almost everyone else. But he operated as part of a much larger, multinational organization. Each time he secured a client, he did so by making promises that people from every other division of the company (compliance and risk, manufacturing, supply chain, design, etc.) had to deliver on. Whenever one of these divisions told him that something wasn't possible or that it went against the broader company strategy, he lashed out. He accused them of not understanding the importance of the US market, berated them for not seeing that he was right, and tried to bully them into going along with his solutions.

All those departments also dealt with country heads from around the world, and over time, they became less responsive to Olivier. Because nobody liked working with him, Olivier fell down the informal pecking order, which made it even harder for him to deliver on his promises. This quickly became a negative-feedback loop: Olivier responded with even more self-righteous indignation, and the other departments responded even less. Everyone at headquarters and in the other bureaus thought Olivier was an arrogant jerk, and he thought that they were idiots for trying to butt in on his business when the US arm was finally, for the first time, performing well.

We heard all of the above from Olivier during our first meeting with him, when we let him go on a 45-minute soliloquy about how the world would be better if everyone recognized how right he was. Then we asked two simple questions: "Was he getting what he needed from his peers?" and "Was he setting himself up to achieve his career aspirations?"

Olivier is smart. And he was open to reflection. Within a minute, he realized that even if everything he said in his 45-minute rant was right, he was being completely ineffective in achieving what he wanted. From this awareness, Olivier began to shift his mindset from right/wrong to being effective. On the other side of the pond, our colleague did the same work with headquarters and the other bureaus to help them see that even if they were right about Olivier, they were not being effective. Through this shift in their mindsets, Oliver and his colleagues came together for a real dialogue about how they could best work together. They found new ways to collaborate while still establishing boundaries that left Olivier with enough autonomy to leverage his natural strengths.

Encouraging Creativity and Ownership

Economist and statistician E. F. Schumacher proposed in his book *A Guide for the Perplexed*[2] that for all the challenges we face, there are only two fundamental kinds of problems in the world—convergent and divergent problems. *Convergent* problems have only one answer, such as the answer to "What is 1 + 1?" *Divergent* problems, in contrast, have infinite possible answers. The longer we spend on divergent problems, the more potential solutions we find. Almost every significant problem a team faces is a divergent problem. Some examples include:

- Who should we hire?
- How can we best address a team member with a bad attitude?
- What projects should our team prioritize (or deprioritize) for the next six months?
- What training program should we invest in given how busy we are?

Let's take a hypothetical example of a team of four leaders in a risk and compliance division. Karen, who leads the compliance department, lost an employee eight months ago and still doesn't have a replacement. Since then, her team has struggled with its workload. Karen says that she needs a new worker or else the people who are still there will burn out and quit. Jack, who heads risk, feels that Karen's ask is completely unreasonable. He thinks that he needs the new hire more because he has *two* open positions in his group, and the team is about to do a company-wide risk audit. Thomas leads the information technology (IT) team and thinks that this is the wrong conversation entirely and that they should focus on automating and streamlining processes. Cynthia, the head of the risk and compliance division, just heard from the CEO that she has to cut one more employee from her department as part of a company-wide cost-cutting effort.

The team faces a problem—it needs to reduce costs without losing effectiveness at a time when most people feel like they need more support. There is no single right answer to this case, but if Cynthia (who has the most power) approached it from a right/wrong mindset, as if it were a convergent problem, she might just rationalize that because Jack's department is more diminished than Karen's, she needs to make the cut to Karen's team. Cynthia would then inform her team of her decision, tell the team to accept it, and move along, even though Karen and Jack both asked her for more people, not fewer. In this case, the rest of the team wouldn't feel listened to or respected, and over time, resentment would build and the team would stop giving its input.

If Cynthia approached the same problem from an effectiveness mindset and asked herself and her team how they could cut costs *while* supporting Jack and Karen, she and her team might find other solutions. Cynthia also would be including Jack and Karen in the decision-making process, which would grant them a sense of ownership over whatever solution they came up with. Maybe Thomas has a way to automate enough of Karen's processes that she actually wouldn't mind losing another worker. Perhaps through a full audit of the team's processes, they find a way to streamline them so that a position in Jack's department is no long necessary. Maybe they discover that IT's budget is a little bloated, and they can eliminate a job there without making severe sacrifices. This approach significantly improves the creativity of the team—instead of competing, they can work together to try to find a solution within the constraints they have.

And notice something—none of the ideas are what any one person thinks is the "perfect choice." Karen and Jack each still want a new employee, and Thomas wants to be talking about something else entirely. But they are all codeveloping solutions that, while imperfect to each member of the team, are at least something they can all get behind. Perfect cannot be the enemy of good. Looking for a perfect solution, even if you enlist the help of others, is still a dysfunctional right/wrong mindset–based behavior. All too often the perfect answer doesn't exist. The optimal answer is a not-so-perfect solution but one that everyone accepts, buys into, and can move forward with.

Returning to our hypothetical example, there's always a chance that even after having these conversations, Cynthia realizes that she has to cut a position from Karen's team and that they can't replace that worker with automation. Some might ask, "Why go through so much conversation and debate if you just do what you were always going to do?" The difference is that in the process, Cynthia proves to her team that she cares and that she is willing to expend her own energy to help them overcome their challenges. The message is much closer to "We will overcome these constraints and figure out how to thrive" instead of "This is how it has to be. I want you to make it work." This might sound like a minor distinction, but it could be the difference between buy-in from Karen and Karen quitting in protest and frustration.

Imagine a jazz ensemble with everyone in the right/wrong mindset. When one player introduces a new theme or an unexpected riff, everyone else on stage stops playing. Or maybe everyone else plays louder and tries to drown out the new theme. It would be a disaster. The ensemble would never find a flow, and everything would collapse into dissonance and cacophony.

Any jazz improviser worth his or her salt lives in the effectiveness mindset. In that mindset, if a bandmate tries something new, instead of sulking or competing, everyone else explores it. Even if at first the theme feels clunky, the bandmates play, add flourishes, and try to find the beauty and complexity in the theme—and more often than not they do. But when they don't, they can all agree to move along, without assigning blame or making the musician who made the original attempt wrong.

The same dynamic exists in a team where everyone lives the effectiveness mindset. Team members listen to each other. They approach each situation with openness. They try to find value in every bad situation, in every half-formed idea. Everyone can play with each other. We don't mean play in a silly way (jazz musicians are deathly serious about how they play). We mean that people can explore and develop ideas in a creative, collaborative, free-flowing way—together.

From Label to Label to Human to Human

Humans apply labels to one another in an attempt to process and understand the world. We use a great diversity of labels. They can be as simple as a role-based label, such as chief technology officer, shop floor worker, supervisor, manager, director, or vice president. We also use functional labels that describe the work a person does, such as sales, marketing, IT, human resources, or project lead. Then there are the more subjective, interpretative labels, ones that make assumptions about capability, such as reliable/unreliable, creative/predictable, or expert/novice, or character labels, such as tough, caring, inspirational, rude, fun, or aloof.

Labels serve a purpose—they're a social shorthand that helps us act in appropriate ways around different people. Interacting with a boss, for instance, requires a different style of communication than interacting with a customer, a friend, or a subordinate. Labels also make it easier to describe how the world works. We don't say, "A previously unknown human being who will soon oversee my work and determine if I will be promoted or fired just came into our office to learn more about how it works." We say, "The new boss just arrived."

This shorthand also has three major downsides:

1. **On teams that are tied to labels, everybody responds to the preconceived notions those labels invoke instead of to what actually happens in a situation.** Returning to the statement, "The new boss just arrived," the phrase *new boss* will conjure a different meaning for and a different reaction from each person in the

office. One person might think that he or she needs to go out of his or her way to show the new boss respect. Another might expect the new boss to fire some employees, so that person might start acting in an extrasafe, conservative way to preserve his or her job. This not only creates dysfunction, but it wastes time. New bosses have to dispel what everyone believes about them before they can even connect with their team.

2. **Labeling dehumanizes people and creates transactional relationships.** We often hear frontline workers gripe, "I am just a number." By this they mean, "I am just a thing, a resource to be used and discarded." Labels often reduce people to the level of a utility. In the corporate world, this can be convenient, especially when it is time to make difficult decisions. But it is also tremendously disempowering for individual employees. It limits how that individual shows up within the team and it prevents that individual from sharing all his or her diverse capabilities, ideas, and experiences. In other words, it prevents the team from exploring its collective infinite potential.

One of the most dehumanizing and common labels we hear in organizations is "us" and "them." People often label their own tribe as "us" and outsiders as "them." Us, the employees, versus them, the managers; us, production, versus them, maintenance; us, management, versus them, the shareholders. Whenever we hear these words, we know that the company has a dysfunctional relationship with fear. It's often a sign that people see their colleagues as threats rather than as collaborators who can help them grow.

3. **When we view labels as fixed, they prevent us from learning new things about ourselves and other people.** It's important to remember that we label ourselves as much as we do others. Often we don't interact with the people around us; rather, we interact with the labels we've assigned to them from the labels we've assigned ourselves. We assume that we know everything about this person—who she is, how she'll show up, what she'll

say, how she'll treat us and why, how she deserves to be treated and why, etc. Likewise, we assume that we know everything about ourselves. Labels wreck the magic of new possibilities in relationships and doom us to repeat our old, dysfunctional patterns.

To counter this, we need to interact with each other human to human. We need to keep an open and curious mind about the people we meet and about what drives them so as to understand that there's wonderful complexity and mystery within everyone. In this human-to-human mindset, we acknowledge that we can't see inside someone else's mind and that we can only discover what that person thinks through conversation. We believe that everyone can contribute in magnificent ways that we cannot imagine and that everyone can learn to adopt new patterns and mindsets. Nobody is fixed. We are all works in progress.

> *Nobody is fixed. We are all works in progress.*

The idea is not to do away with labels. Simply put, we treat people as human when we acknowledge that any label is incomplete, limiting, and often inaccurate. We treat people as human when we hold labels lightly rather than as a statement of immutable fact, when we believe that everyone deserves the same respect, regardless of their labels, when we acknowledge that our fundamental needs as human beings don't change depending on our roles and that even the "big boss" needs to feel connected, listened to, and respected, just like the frontline workers serving customers—and indeed just like customers themselves.

This human-to-human frame is the starting point for empathy, deep listening, and trust. It's what allows for principles such as "respect every individual" to be a lived reality, not just an abstract concept. When a team lives human to human, not only do team members know each other's utility but they also know their dreams, aspirations, and histories.

Such teams allow everyone to show up as their whole selves, to feel safe and comfortable contributing new ideas and doing their best. They can adapt, respond, and grow—together.

Action Learning

Teams with the effectiveness and human-to-human mindsets are more likely to step out of the fear archetypes into the unfear archetypes. But the mindsets alone aren't enough. We need to translate these mindsets into actions and skills. The two main skills for team members is building trust and having difficult conversations.

Unfear Practice 1: Building Trust

Trust is like a fragile ecosystem. It enables incredible connection and productivity, but it can be destroyed in the blink of an eye. Once destroyed, it is exceptionally difficult to rebuild. Our hesitation to trust comes, in part, from our evolutionary survival mechanisms. In the plains and forests where humans first evolved, such caution saved lives. In the modern workplace, this fear of trusting others (and ourselves) causes tremendous waste. The two mindset shifts described in this chapter will help you see other people as full, complex humans and to view them with less judgment and more kindness, which will help trust flourish. But you will always encounter and work with people who don't share these mindsets, yet you will need to build trust with them all the same. While it can be more difficult, these four practices will help you build trust, even in the most challenging of circumstances: reliability, acceptance, openness, and authenticity.

Reliability

Reliable people do what they say they will do. Reliability is perhaps the most tangible aspect of trust. Here are the most important ways to improve your reliability:

- **Do not overstate your capability or expertise.** When you admit to your limitations, it might feel like you're selling yourself short. But if you exaggerate what you can accomplish and then under-deliver, it will have severe long-term implications on whether people feel they can trust you.
- **Plan and align.** Be clear about your priorities, and keep all stake-holders regularly informed about your plan.
- **Avoid surprises.** If you know that you are going to miss a deadline or commitment, inform all stakeholders well in advance so that they can plan for the missed deadline. Last-minute surprises create more waste and chaos and significantly detract from trust.
- **Master the effective no.** Saying yes to everything is a surefire way of being either unreliable or exceptionally stressed and over-worked. Ask people to help you prioritize. When dealing with competing requests, bring both parties into a room to have them sort out priorities.

Acceptance

Let's say that you're driving down the freeway and somebody cuts you off. You honk and call the person a jerk. Then you notice that they're driving a BMW, and you think to yourself, "Of course, only entitled jerks who cut other people off drive BMWs." This is an example of a psychological process called *attribution bias*, in which we see the bad behavior of others and make sweeping claims about their intentions and character traits. But we never go through the same process with our-selves. We know that we're good people, and if we ever cut someone off, we only did it for the right reasons. In short, we often judge others based on their worst behavior but judge ourselves based on our best intentions. This same process plays out in business. To return to the Olivier exam-ple, he thought everyone else was wrong and that they were "stupid" and "controlling." When we judge people like this, we destroy trust and wreck relationships, which, in turn, undermines the long-term perfor-mance and well-being of a team.

The way to shift out of this judgment is to practice accepting people for who they are. This doesn't mean that you need to accept poor behavior. You learn to separate people from their behaviors and accept them for who they are, even when you disagree with their behavior. In other words, do not make people wrong for their poor behavior. An acceptance orientation allows you to engage in the most difficult conversations effectively and to give and receive feedback that helps people adjust their poor behaviors into something more effective—all the while building trust.

> We often judge others based on their worst behavior but judge ourselves based on our best intentions.

This is possible because acceptance makes people less defensive, more open to feedback, and more willing to collaborate on new solutions. This happened for Olivier. He learned to stop judging other people in the organization. Instead of thinking of them as stupid and controlling for trying to get involved with his operations, he learned to understand their perspective and why the limits they put on him exist. He accepted them as people, even though he continued to disagree with them. From that place, they engaged in dialogue toward a solution that worked for both parties.

Openness
When people are open, they are willing to be vulnerable and to give and receive feedback. Few things build trust like vulnerability, yet people usually avoid being the first to show vulnerability out of fear that they will make a fool of themselves or get taken advantage of. To facilitate trust in a team, we often ask leaders to share the stories of their lives as well as items of personal significance. Once, a senior leader of an oil refinery spoke about his insulin pump, which he had been wearing as a type 1 diabetic since he was six years old. He shared how this pump had

shaped him as a person. After that, the rest of the team shared their own unique stories. This shifted them from being just colleagues to being a tight-knit group that will always have each other's backs.

Openness in a team context goes beyond vulnerability. It is also about the willingness and ability to give and receive feedback. Giving feedback is a skill. The most important thing to remember is to always give feedback from a place of care and a desire to help. Otherwise, the person might feel attacked and nitpicked. Similarly, there is a skill to receiving feedback. To make feedback useful, you need to hear it accurately, process it, and internalize it. This is impossible if you're defensive. Try to remember how hard it is for the other person to give the feedback. Feel care for that person, feel the care that person put into his or her words, and receive it as a gift rather than punishment.

> *Give feedback from a place*
> *of care and a desire to help.*

Authenticity

People are authentic when what they say and do aligns with what they feel and think. Inauthenticity may win the moment (you don't want to upset someone or you're trying to please multiple people), but it inevitably destroys trust in the long run. People will start to view you as duplicitous.

A word of caution: when openness and authenticity come from a self-orientation and/or a victim mindset, they can break trust. Imagine that you are enraged by a colleague and you scream at him. You might say that you are being authentic, so it should build trust. But it does the opposite because your behavior is focused only on how you are feeling and does not consider the feelings of the other person—likewise if you share a vulnerable story to manipulate others into feeling bad for you or to explain why you dropped the ball or why you lashed out against someone else.

Unfear Practice 2: Having Difficult Conversations

In their book, *Language and Pursuit of Leadership Excellence*,[3] Chalmers Brothers and Vinay Kumar share a story about a child who goes with her father to the office on "Take Your Child to Work Day." When the child comes home, her mother asks what she thought of her dad's job. The child just makes a face. After some prodding from her mother, the child complains that all Daddy does is talk, talk, and talk—on the phone, on his computer, and in meetings with other people.

The kid is right. Most of us spend the majority of our time at work in conversation. Because of this, the quality of a team's conversations *directly* impacts the team's outcomes. The highest-performing teams are those that can best have difficult conversations. We define a *difficult conversation* as any interaction where we care deeply about its impact on ourselves, other people, or some objective or outcome. This can include speaking up for yourself, delivering feedback, disagreeing with a boss or a peer, challenging a norm or the status quo, and multiple other topics.

In many ways, these conversations are the most important things a team does because they raise and address important issues that impact the team's performance that otherwise would stay hidden. Teams that are able to have difficult conversations can assess, problem solve, and make creative decisions much more effectively because they leverage the full talents and ideas of all team members.

The four pillars of trust—reliability, acceptance, openness, and authenticity—enable difficult conversations. Likewise, the more skill you gain in having difficult conversations, the easier it will be to build trust with somebody, and thus it creates a mutually reinforcing virtuous cycle.

Difficult conversations can be a highly effective tool to unfear an entire team. Attempting to help people change their mindsets and reframe their relationship with fear can be incredibly challenging. Handled poorly, these conversations can come across as condescending and create defensiveness. Handled well, they become invitations to join you on an unfear journey.

Truly high-performing teams engage in difficult conversations as improvisation—opportunities to create new and different music that can surprise and delight. In contrast, fearful teams avoid these conversations or engage in them poorly, creating dissonance and cacophony. Let's say, for example, a colleague cuts you off in a meeting. He has a habit of doing this, and you want to confront him. But then you start thinking about how he will respond, how that colleague doesn't take criticism well, and after a while you conclude that talking about it will only stir the pot, so you just drop it. Later that same day, that colleague cuts off someone else in another meeting, and you have the same internal conversation. This is the downward spiral of communication in teams where fear operates. It creates perpetual stress, frustration, and interpersonal friction. All of this degrades performance and well-being.

Even if they avoid the conversations, everybody, on some level, knows that these conversations need to happen. In our workshops, when we ask our clients about the difficult conversations in their workplace, either those they had or those they avoided, we fill up several flip chart pages in minutes. Before you can learn how to get better at these conversations, it's important to know what actually happens in difficult conversations and the typical pitfalls that make them so difficult.

Three Levels of Conversation

We've all been burned by conversations that went wrong, but we can't always identify exactly what went wrong. We believe that we are having one conversation when, in fact, we are having three conversations at once. In their book, *Difficult Conversations: How to Discuss What Matters Most*,[4] Douglas Stone, Bruce Patton, and Sheila Heen explain that each conversation occurs at three distinct levels: facts, feelings, and identity.

The *facts* conversation is the one that we often think we're having. This is where we discuss the details of a situation, what we see happening, what we want to change, and so on.

The *feelings* conversation happens beneath this. All the emotions we are experiencing are part of this conversation. Often, and especially in organizations with a dysfunctional relationship with fear, we either suppress our feelings (for fear of expressing them badly) or we express them poorly.

The *identity* conversation happens beneath this layer. These are the stories people tell themselves about who they are. Often conversations are difficult because they pose a threat to these identities. According to Douglas Stone, Bruce Patton, and Sheila Heen,[5] the three main identities we hold for ourselves in the workplace are: (1) I'm a nice person, (2) I'm a competent person, and (3) I'm worthy of love and respect. Many of us tend to hold one of these more tightly than the others. For example, Fault Finders, Competitors, Perfectionists, and Avoiders tend to identify with "I'm competent," whereas Controllers and Minions tend to identify with "I'm worthy of love and respect," and rule followers and likables tend to believe "I'm a nice person."

These are not hard and fast rules. We hold these identities and express these archetypes in a variety of ways. The point is that this is all taking place *beneath the waterline*. Where we have the most doubt or fear is where we are most likely to cling to an identity. Am I really a competent person? The more I question this and assume that it's important for me to be safe and secure in this world, the more likely I am to be triggered by something or someone who challenges this.

For example, I (Mark) am a bit too wrapped up in "being competent." I've held onto the story that access to success, safety, and happiness in life is to be found in being competent and competing favorably against others. This has served me well, but it has also levied a steep cost. I start to see threats or challenges to my competence wherever I look, and it's also very easy for me to believe that others feel a desire to be competent as well. Now, if I attempt to give some difficult feedback to someone with an "I'm worthy of respect" identity, it can go south fast. With the best of intentions, I may provide lots of helpful feedback for this person, but he or she might completely shut down because of his or her deepest fear of not being worthy of respect has just been provoked. This person's priority is to feel embraced, not corrected. The person might then lash out at me, perhaps attacking my own competence, which would then likely trigger an amygdala hijack within myself. Soon the conversation deteriorates, we both walk away, and neither of us knows what exactly went wrong because we didn't pay attention to the emotions and stories about identity that simmered beneath the surface of our conversation.

Another form of identity that needs to be considered when engaging in difficult conversations is related to race, gender, and sexual orientation. When we ignore these aspects in our difficult conversations, we fail to take into account the different lenses from which people might be looking at the same situation and how they, based on their own experiences, might interpret what you say.

We need to learn how to effectively manage our conversations on all three levels. All communication, of course, is a two-way street. We have to first master reflective listening so that we can understand what is happening in our conversations before we learn how to speak our truth.

Practice Reflective Listening

Listening and hearing are two distinct things. Hearing is a purely biological process. We can hear without comprehending—in fact, we do it all the time. To truly comprehend, we must *listen*, which means tuning in and remaining present in a conversation. This is because listening, unlike hearing, doesn't function on a purely biological level. When we listen to another person speak, we rely on our mindsets to interpret the words they say. If we aren't conscious of how our mindsets impact our perspective, then we can walk away from the conversation with a completely different understanding of what was said than our interlocutor.

The key to reflective, deep listening is to listen in order to be effective. When we listen to be effective, we come into a conversation with the intention to truly understand what the other person says. We come in open to the possibility that we may be wrong, that we may not have all the information, and that the other person may surprise us. Essentially, we arrive with a deep level of curiosity for what the other person will say and a desire to understand the conversation on all three levels: facts, feelings, and identities. When we come in with this mindset, we can practice reflective listening, a technique laid out by William Miller and Stephen Rollnick in their book, *Motivational Interviewing*.[6]

The essence of a reflective listening response is that it makes a guess about what the person means. Before a person speaks, he or she has a certain meaning to communicate. The meaning is encoded into words, often imperfectly. People don't always say exactly what they mean. The listener has to hear the words accurately and then decode their meaning.

Reflective listening, then, is a process of decoding and clarification. It's hearing what the other person says, reading the person's nonverbal cues, processing both, and then checking that the way we interpreted both is correct. When we do this well, after a few back-and-forths, a shared meaning evolves in which both parties have the same understanding of the issue in question.

> *When we listen to be effective, we come into a conversation with the intention to truly understand what the other person says. We come in open to the possibility that we may be wrong, that we may not have all the information, and that the other person may surprise us. Essentially, we arrive with a deep level of curiosity for what the other person will say and a desire to understand the conversation on all three levels: facts, feelings, and identities.*

Let's take a relatively simple example. Hypothetically, you ask a colleague to make sure that she reads all the materials that she needs to before each meeting. The colleague respond, "Okay, I'll try." You sense some emotion in her voice. If you simply listen for a factual understanding, you might respond, "Great, thanks," but if you're reflectively listening, you might realize that something else is going on and say, "Thanks for offering that, but I'm sensing that you have a challenge or concern we haven't addressed yet." From there, your colleague has an opportunity to clarify what that emotion was. Maybe she feels swamped, or perhaps she only received the materials 20 minutes before the meeting and needs more time. Whatever it is, if there's no follow-up, it remains her private meaning. When you reflectively listen and invite more dialogue, it draws that meaning out, becomes shared, and allows you to potentially help your colleague with her challenge.

The benefits to reflective listening are immense. Without it, learning in relationships just isn't possible. With it, people can persist in difficult conversations and do so in a way that builds trust, deepens relationships, and generates new insights that didn't exist before.

Speak Your Truth so That Others Can Hear It

We often live in the dilemma of sharing what's on our mind directly and truthfully or mollifying and suppressing what we really think. This, however, is a false dichotomy. We don't just have to share our truth in a toxic way or suppress it. The other choice is to learn to speak our truth effectively, in a way that doesn't contribute to fear and dysfunction on a team. There are two maxims for speaking your truth effectively: own your perspective and be respectful:

Own Your Perspective. The first part of speaking effectively in difficult conversations is learning to speak from a place of ownership. This might seem like a simple thing—just say what you mean!—but it goes much deeper than that. When we are truly taking ownership, we speak from a position of knowledge about what's in our own minds and are clear about what we don't fully know. And ultimately, there's only one thing that we can speak directly about: our own perspective. Owning our perspective means that we acknowledge that our points of view and our interpretations are inherently limited. We don't hold our views as absolute truth because they aren't.

> *We tend to live as if the fictions unfolding inside our minds are really facts that are evident for everyone else to see. Clear thinking is not rejecting these fictions but seeing them for what they are—our perspective, not the perspective.*

To understand what we mean, we have to talk about the difference between observation and interpretation. An *observation* is a statement of fact, verifiable by others. Our *interpretation* is the meaning that we give that fact. A truly clear-minded and epistemically humble person recognizes that his or her interpretations aren't inherently true or complete and acknowledges this in conversation. These people also recognize that they will always have more to learn about a situation. People who are misguided or fooling themselves will state their interpretation as fact and cling to it.

Said differently, we tend to live as if the fictions unfolding inside our minds are really facts that are evident for everyone else to see. Clear thinking is not rejecting these fictions but seeing them for what they are—*our* perspective, not *the* perspective.

To have effective difficult conversations, therefore, we must learn to separate observation from interpretation. This is harder than it sounds. Let's have a little quiz. Which of these statements are interpretations and which are observations?

- "That meeting went way too long."
- "You made a great point."

- "You're late, again."
- "We had a very positive quarter with 10 percent growth in sales."
- "You didn't let me finish my point."
- "The meeting started at five minutes past the hour."

The last statement is the only observation. Every one of the other statements is an interpretation because they all have assumptions built into them. What does *too long* mean? What's a *great point*? Who's to say that the 10 percent growth in sales is *very positive*?

To open a conversation with any of these statements without acknowledging that they are interpretations could lead to trouble. Communicators who take ownership of their perspective use versions of this phrase: "I observed [blank]. From that I interpreted [blank]. Is that accurate?" For example, instead of saying, "That meeting went way too long," you can say "The meeting ended 20 minutes past schedule. When this happens, I interpret this as meaning that our team isn't working very efficiently. How do others see it?"

It might feel silly to use this language for something that seems relatively small. But it is vital to build this habit of communication so that in more pressing and stressful situations you don't revert to a more toxic, interpretation-as-fact style in the midst of an amygdala hijack. Using this language is a powerful way to deliver a message to others without making them wrong. You're not offering your interpretation as a statement of objective truth; you're offering your interpretation. Given a dialogue and new information, you could very well change how you see things.

> *To effectively enter a learning conversation,*
> *we must separate observation from*
> *interpretation, cold facts about the world*
> *from colorful and vital fictions in our mind.*

Your interpretation isn't the end of the conversation—it's simply the starting point. Own it but hold it lightly. Stay curious, and update your interpretation as you learn more.

Be Respectful. When speaking, we all have a responsibility to package our thoughts in words that can be received easily. If someone asks you what you think about a project and you say, "My interpretation is that it sucks," you may be honest, but you're not being respectful. This response would likely trigger an amygdala hijack in the other person, make that person defensive, and completely ruin any chance of productive communication.

To be respectful, we need to share the values and concerns that have led us to the interpretation that we've made. In other words, we have to speak to the feelings and identity levels of the conversation. So, instead of saying that the project sucks, share what values are at stake and what concerns you have. You may value the opportunity to provide input on the project and share your thoughts openly, even if they're not popular opinions. You may value the team and company putting time and resources into successful projects, but don't want to see the company waste money on failing ones. In terms of concerns, you may be concerned that the team is throwing good money after bad. Or perhaps the team hasn't applied the lessons learned from the last project that didn't go so well.

What's important to keep in mind is that these are your values and your concerns, and they've led to your own interpretation. You own them. You're not projecting a toxic interpretation of events onto other people. You're simply expressing what's important to you. And your interpretation is so important that you want to share it, without judgment and blame, with others.

Now, when your boss asks for your opinion, you can tap into your values and concerns and share them: "Thank you for giving me the opportunity to share my views. Making sure this project is successful is important to me, and I think it's critical that the company makes good use of limited resources. I'm concerned that this project is not on the right track, and we haven't been able to make use of the lessons learned from the last project on this one." This statement is honest and respectful. You say what you mean, you don't make anybody wrong for what has happened, and you create the space for a learning dialogue.

This is what difficult conversations are all about: learning to say what you mean while giving people room to say what they mean. It's like a jazz musician who learns how to play his own instrument and then makes sure to leave room for the rest of the ensemble to contribute their notes. Let the music begin.

> *Say what you mean, don't make anybody wrong for what has happened, and create the space for a learning dialogue.*

WORTH THINKING ABOUT

- How might you be showing up with a mindset of right/wrong in your relationships?

- What labels do you place on yourself or others? How might these be limiting your ability to build effective relationships?

- Think of one strained relationship you have at work:

  ○ How much trust exists in this relationship? Which pillar of trust needs most work in this relationship? What tangible actions can you take to strengthen this pillar?

  ○ Are you engaging in the necessary difficult conversations or avoiding them? How can you engage in these conversations more effectively?

7

The Unfear Organization

Embarking on a Journey with a Thousand Heroes

One of the defining aspects of humanity is our yearning to make sense of the world through myths and storytelling. In his book *A Hero with a Thousand Faces*,[1] Joseph Campbell argues that this cross-cultural desire has given rise to what he calls the "Hero's Journey." This is an archetypal story in which the hero or heroine leaves the comfort and certainty of home and sets off on an epic journey to unknown lands and worlds. Along the way, the hero meets friends, allies, and mentors. The hero also goes through trials and tribulations. The hero is challenged to examine his or her beliefs and overcome tremendous difficulty to return home safe, triumphant, and changed by the dangers he or she has faced. In the end, the hero has acquired new wisdom and a fresh perspective on life. Think of Luke Skywalker in *Star Wars* leaving the comfortable yet monotonous life he had on Tatooine to, quite unexpectedly, become a Jedi and join the Rebel Alliance in its fight against Darth Vader and the Empire. Think of Odysseus returning from Troy. Think of Harry Potter and Hermione Granger battling Lord Voldemort. Think of the origin story of your country or organization.

Humans apply this same desire for meaning-making to their own lives. We view ourselves as heroes, and we discover more about ourselves as we go on these journeys.

An unfear organization is a journey with a thousand heroes. Each person within the organization is a hero in their own right, undergoing their own individual challenges and transformations. An unfear organization brings a group of these heroes together, gives them the equipment and skills they need on their journey, and, vitally, helps them develop the courage and resilience necessary to make it through the belly of the beast. In this way, the organization transforms its people and also the world around it.

Transformational Learning

Most people don't think of organizations as having mindsets, but they do. The people who make up an organization can hold a collective mindset. That collectively held belief can impact the mindsets of the individuals within. Because of the nature of mindsets, it can be more difficult to change a collective mindset than an individual one. It requires buy-in from far more people. That said, any leader (which, because we are all leaders, means any employee) can start a transformation that changes the collective mindset. Of course, some leaders have more sway in an organization than others, but the amount of influence you have is not always determined by your position in the hierarchy. To create an unfear transformation at an organizational level, you need to build a coalition and get people above and below you to adopt the mindsets and to pick up the practices that will unfear an organization.

There are four mindsets to start with:

- From stretch through fear to stretch through purpose
- From parent-child to adult-adult
- From vertical to horizontal thinking
- From defense of the status quo to continuous evolution

From Stretch Through Fear
to Stretch Through Purpose

For an organization to achieve ever-improving performance, it must create a desire within employees to stretch—to move beyond their current condition and achieve something greater. In his seminal book, *The Fifth Discipline*, Peter Senge describes stretch this way: "Imagine a rubber band, stretched between your vision and current reality. When stretched, the rubber band creates tension, representing the tension between vision and current reality. What does the tension seek? Resolution or release."[2]

There are only two ways the tension can be resolved. Either vision pulls reality toward it, creating growth, or reality pulls vision toward it, maintaining the status quo or even causing a contraction (Figure 7.1).

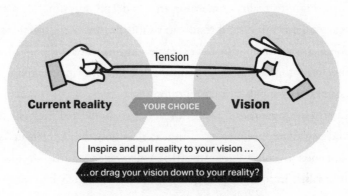

FIGURE 7.1   Current reality versus vision

Traditional fear-based organizations hold the mindset that the best way to create stretch is to focus on the current reality. What this means in practical terms is that such organizations constantly talk about the demerits and negative consequences of the current reality. They attempt to use fear about negative consequences to light a fire under the workers' you-know-whats. The basic form of this mindset is, "Bad stuff will happen unless we [do something or avoid something]," "I will lose my job unless I perform better," "We will lose market share unless we cut prices," and so on. The organization conflates success with avoiding negative short-term consequences instead of building long-term success. Because the focus is on merely surviving reality, the stretch is usually resolved by the vision moving closer to reality rather than the other way around.

This belief, of course, is grounded in reality. Bad things can and do happen. Markets crash. Economies sputter. Consumer demand shifts. New Competitors arise. We make mistakes. We miss project deadlines. And because this mindset is fear based, it spurs rapid action in the short term as people respond to crises with more energy than they do when things are normal. However, it also has a tremendous detrimental impact.

First, burning platforms create desperation, not aspiration. Desperation keeps organizations and their heroes stuck in survival mode. No one created great organizations out of desperation to avoid negative consequences. Organizations are created when people have the aspiration to bring into reality something that is deeply meaningful to them. Fear narrows our minds and results in simplistic, knee-jerk reactions that provide a short-term boost: for example, cutting costs with no thought to long term consequences to improve the bottom line or giving cash incentives to boost end-of-quarter sales.

In extreme cases, these simplistic reactions can lead to dishonest actions to avoid negative consequences. This is exactly how the "Dieselgate" scandal happened at Volkswagen. In 2015, Volkswagen was the world's largest automaker. Everything was going great. Then the US Environmental Protection Agency (EPA) slapped the company with a violation of the Clean Air Act because it had artificially lowered NOx emissions in laboratory tests to meet US standards. It was revealed that the company's turbocharged direct injection diesel engines emitted up to 40 times more NOx in real-world driving. The company's stock price fell by a third. The Group CEO Martin Winterkorn and many senior leaders were dismissed or resigned. The company reported its first quarterly loss in more than 15 years, and by June 2020, the scandal had cost Volkswagen more than $33 billion in fines, penalties, financial settlements, and buyback costs.

Somewhere along the way, delivering profit became paramount. The easy interpretation is to dismiss Volkswagen's leadership as morally corrupt. In our experience, however, very few people are inherently corrupt. Rather, they behave in corrupt ways in response to an obsessive focus on profit and shareholder value. They're motivated by fear to deliver the top- or bottom-line number and believe that cutting corners is preferable to facing immediate negative outcomes.

Used repeatedly, this creating stretch through fear mindset leads to the *cry wolf syndrome.* Employees stop believing their leaders when they claim that the company is facing yet another crisis. Instead of cohesion and focus, it leads to second-guessing, indifference, and wasteful internal politics. Employees become immune to the messaging, so the organization screams louder and creates even greater panic to break through.

Unfear organizations, in contrast, create stretch by focusing on the *vision.* And this is key—they create a vision that encapsulates a greater sense of purpose, a positive, meaningful impact that the company makes on the world. When employees feel connected to a higher purpose, it helps them step into their unfear selves because they find a sense of meaning and joy in their work. They move the current reality toward the vision because they feel inspired to put their creative best into each project. From there, they are much more likely to embrace fear as a cue for learning.

> *Creating stretch through fear wears employees down. Meaning and purpose enable the optimistic stretch that helps employees deal with everyday challenges with greater buoyancy.*

That said, companies cannot ignore profit. Profit is what allows a business to continue to exist, grow, and invest in new operations and ideas. Organizations then have to live in a sort of paradox, where they simultaneously manage to survive day-to-day life while still working toward a higher purpose.

A critical task of leadership, therefore, is to inject the organizational space with meaning and purpose that creates the optimistic stretch needed to deal with everyday challenges. One great example of this is the music publisher Kobalt Music Group. You may not have heard of Kobalt, but you probably engage with the music it oversees every day. Company founder Willard Ahdritz started the company with the explicit purpose of giving more power to artists. Traditional music publishers provide very little compensation to artists, and they also have opaque processes so that artists aren't always sure where their music is being sold and for how much.

Ahdritz created a business that was the opposite of this. He instituted total transparency by allowing the creators to see the metrics on their songs in one app. He also honored his commitment to pay artists more. There are several other ways that Ahdritz built a creator-friendly platform, but the big takeaway is that he created a company that did more than pay lip service to its purpose. It lived it. And the company has been hugely successful. In 2019, Kobalt represented 38 of the top 100 artists on US radio, and the company's revenues have climbed year after year.

In our conversation with Ahdritz, he credited his commitment to purpose as a key driver of his success. He pointed out that Kobalt is a company of about 700 people with an average age of 30 years. These people joined the company because of the purpose: they want to empower creators. It's part of why Ahdritz has been able to attract top talent to the company and inspire them to perform at a high level.

We think the Kobalt story is instructive for organizations. Profit without purpose rarely creates excitement and often throws the entire system into a state of fear. When the energy of the organizational space is primarily oriented toward profit, it suggests that the organization's purpose is merely to survive and not do anything greater. Such a survival orientation perpetuates fear archetypes with all the accompanying dysfunction. Creating stretch through purpose is the better, more sustainable approach.

From Parent-Child to Adult-Adult

Do you want a thousand heroes in your organization or a thousand children? Leaders in most fear-based organizations view their subordinates as children. They think that without strict control and coddling, nobody will get any work done. They institute harsh limits, build rigid structures, and give orders. They also believe that only those higher up in the corporate hierarchy have the intelligence and ability to make significant decisions or solve major problems. Instead of letting employees develop and test their own solutions, these leaders step in the moment they think their employee is stuck. Most organizations, however, do not realize that they operate from this mindset.

Usually, this mindset and behavior come from the best of intentions. Just as parents want the best for their children, these leaders want the best for their employees. They think that these limits help employees achieve and keep them safe. In reality, this mindset leads organizations to waste the incredible potential of their heroes because they don't even recognize that potential. It stifles creativity and engagement from the front lines, which prevents companies from leveraging the collective wisdom of all their employees.

In unfear organizations, leaders view their employees as fellow adults and treat them as such. Beyond that, they recognize that everybody can make decisions and can contribute beyond their job description. They understand that everyone is a leader in their own right: we are all the CEOs of our own lives, and the way that we show up and behave in the workplace always has an effect on how other people act. In these organizations, leaders don't micromanage, use fear to motivate, or coddle their workers. Instead, they focus on creating the conditions for people to do their work and find new ways to improve that work.

In the adult-to-adult mindset, leaders lead with humility. Instead of thinking of themselves as superior, as the only adults in the relationship, they recognize the ability and potential of everyone around them. Because of this, leaders feel more comfortable delegating decisions and inviting broad dialogue when facing adversity and challenges. They recognize that everyone has something to teach them, so they start to learn from the collective wisdom of their colleagues. Leaders also don't feel the need to be overprotective of their employees' feelings. When they have feedback to give, they give it in a straightforward (but respectful) manner.

> *In the adult-to-adult mindset, leaders lead with humility. Instead of thinking of themselves as superior, as the only adults in the relationship, they recognize the ability and potential of everyone around them. They also don't feel the need to be overprotective of their employees' feelings.*

Toyota does a fabulous job of embodying the adult-to-adult mindset. The company treats all its employees as adults, trusts them to make decisions, and expects them to contribute new ideas and innovations to the company. The company backs up this mindset with plenty of concrete actions. For example, think back to the *andon* cord we discussed in Chapter 4. When an employee pulls that cord, it stops production to convene a collective problem-solving session, with the manager and other employees coming together to help brainstorm a fix to whatever issue has come up. The very fact that the cord even exists proves that Toyota views its employees as adults. Pulling the *andon* cord can be extremely costly because it stops production for the entire line. The fact that Toyota gives its frontline workers the agency to make this call shows the amount of trust it has in its workers.

In organizations with this mindset, employees feel energized and respected as co-owners of the organization's future. There is no better way to create well-being than treating employees as adults. In Chapter 5 we discussed the infinite potential of an individual. When organizations break the parent-child paradigm and move to an adult-to-adult paradigm, they create the space for the infinite potential of their thousands of heroes to burst forth and produce unimaginable outcomes.

From Vertical to Horizontal Thinking

In the vertical mindset that most fear-based organizations hold, employees optimize for their departmental or functional objectives, even if it hurts the overall performance of the organization. By way of an example, imagine a soccer team. The offense is incentivized to score goals, and the defense is incentivized to prevent them. If this team had a vertical mindset, the offense would rather lose four to five than win one to nothing because even though the team lost, it scored more goals. Similarly, the defense of this team would rather lose zero to one than win five to four because in the first scenario, it performed better, even if the team lost.

This kind of optimizing for the subsystem at the detriment of the whole frequently plays out in fear-based organizations. For example, one of our clients once had several million dollars of product ready to be packaged and shipped out, but the procurement department—which was responsible for receiving packaging and labels from subcontractors—would not release the packaging materials because of a missing document, even though it knew that the packaging met requirements. The delay cost the company millions of dollars and led to a very unhappy customer. But in its vertical silo, the procurement department had made the right choice because it had done things by the book. We regularly see this mindset play out in sales and fulfillment. Each side thinks only about optimizing for its own objectives instead of thinking holistically about the value chain. Then orders go unfulfilled, and each department blames the other. In the most extreme examples of this mindset, leaders run their organization as fiefdoms and openly compete with other teams or departments.

Unfear organizations, in contrast, operate with a horizontal mindset. In this mindset, instead of trying to just serve the boss, people look for ways to collaborate with different stakeholders to achieve their desired outcomes. This mindset has a major implication for how the organization operates internally and how it interacts with the external world.

Internal Operations

In the horizontal mindset, organizations recognize that the role of leaders is to enable their employees and remove blockages to work instead of acting as checkpoints that everything has to run through. In this mindset, teams and departments collaborate with one another seamlessly to deliver value to customers. To understand just how important this collaboration is, think about any essential output that your organization produces. Then write down the names of all the people and departments involved in its creation. Chances are that you will end up with a long list, with inputs from several departments. Almost everything requires interdepartmental collaboration, and removing even one person or link from that chain will impact the entire system. To return to the procurement example, if the procurement department operated with the horizontal mindset, it would have moved heaven and earth to get the missing document or come up with an alternate creative solution to ensure that packaging was delivered on time.

External Interactions

When organizations hold a truly horizontal mindset, they seek opportunities to partner with all stakeholders—employees, customers, suppliers, sellers, shareholders, and the community—to achieve outcomes that go beyond what any of them could do alone. These organizations become a hub of collaboration and innovation.

For example, Wikipedia realized that it could democratize knowledge by inviting volunteers to write articles. By expanding the boundaries of the organization to include everyone, in a very short time span, the English version of Wikipedia was able to create more than 5 million web articles, and the company accomplished this with only 30 employees. Compare this with *Encyclopedia Britannica*, which relied on highly trained experts to write the articles for its 28-volume sets. The company kept itself siloed off and now has been almost completely replaced by Wikipedia.

Not every organization can operate like Wikipedia, but almost every organization can find opportunities to partner with stakeholders beyond its boundaries. We see it more and more as organizational borders have become more porous and allow collaboration in profound new ways with partners, customers, competitors, and governments. Johnson & Johnson and Merck collaborated to mass produce their Covid-19 vaccine. Tesla made its LINUX coding for the car open source. Twenty-five percent of Procter and Gamble's new products came through crowdsourcing using platforms such as the InnoCentive Network rather than the company's internal research and development department.[3]

From Defense of the Status Quo to Continuous Evolution

Organizations with the defense of the status quo mindset expect employees to focus on just doing their work. They believe that a model employee is one who keeps his or her head down, never questions anything, and gets the work done. In these organizations, thought processes, actions, and systems become entrenched. Nobody asks whether these assumptions or ways of operating actually meet the current challenges the organization faces.

A generation ago, a *Kodak moment* meant something that was worth saving and savoring. Today the term refers to a company being so stuck in the status quo and clinging so hard to its golden goose that it forgets to innovate and loses all relevance. This is exactly what happened to Kodak, which was so enamored with its business model of analog photographs that it completely missed the digital revolution.

Unfear organizations, in contrast, hold a mindset of continuous evolution. In this mindset, the organization expects and encourages employees to learn how to *improve* their work. Vitally, unfear organizations don't focus exclusively on the easy-to-measure metrics. They recognize that mindsets, beliefs, and assumptions often govern the way that people work, and they spend just as much time questioning and improving those mindsets as they do the more tangible processes. They view everyday situations as an opportunity to learn, to find a creative approach, and to change. Organizations that live this mindset have a palpably different feel to them. As soon as you step into these organizations, such as Toyota or Menlo, you immediately encounter vibrant, creative individuals. The teams work on solving problems, making incremental improvements with energy and joy. These little steps forward add up to make a large difference in performance and well-being. All the behaviors at Toyota—the *andon* cords, going to *gemba*, and so on—create a culture of continuous evolution. The company encourages employees to question the status quo and gives them the tools to make improvements.

> *Unfear organizations have a mindset*
> *of continuous evolution.*

When organizations live this mindset, continuous improvement becomes integral to how they operate. Everyone stretches themselves, but they also encourage each other. They realize that the end goal is to create something better and to improve collectively, so they collaborate instead of competing. Leaders encourage their employees to problem solve, and they act more as coaches than as directors. This mindset also helps encourage people to stretch to reach challenging goals.

When the organizational space is infused with these four unfear mindsets, the system overflows with energy and creativity that allows it to thrive and respond effectively to uncertainty. However, infusing these mindsets into a highly complex space full of interdependencies and connections is easier said than done. Let us explore some action learning practices to create and sustain such an organization.

Action Learning

Action learning comes in the form of the tools and skills you give the thousands of heroes in your organization so that they can continue the journey. It is also how you actually make sure to motivate everybody, keep them moving in the same direction, and help them discover the resilience necessary to overcome the challenges they face. While there are infinite ways to equip the heroes, there are four key practices that companies should undertake to bring about an unfear transformation:

- Making the workplace a space for exchanging generative stories and lore
- Creating powerful learning routines that drive both efficiency and effectiveness
- Inspiring through personal and collective action (role modeling)
- Aligning performance management with the unfear culture

Unfear Practice 1: Making the Workplace a Space for Exchanging Generative Stories and Lore

Throughout human history, we have passed down culture from generation to generation through stories—from early cave drawings, to the works of Homer, Dante, and Shakespeare, to Hollywood and Bollywood films. Stories stick with us because they speak simultaneously to our emotions and intellect. Not only do they impact our conscious thought, but they also penetrate deep into our subconscious and shape us. They allow us to become part of something greater than ourselves.

> *Stories stick with us because they speak simultaneously to our emotions and intellect. Not only do they impact our conscious thought, but they also penetrate deep into our subconscious and shape our mental models of how the world works.*

In much the same way that societies share their culture through stories, organizations do as well. Whenever we start working with a new client, we tune into the stories that the employees tell each other about the organization. This gives us the clearest sense of that company's purpose, relationship with fear, history, values, and mindsets.

In fear-based organizations, most people tell stories about losses, breakdowns in trust, the negative consequences of underperformance, us versus them, and so on. They share victim narratives, in which employees and the company alike feel that they are at the mercy of outside forces. These fear-based narratives get so deeply embedded in the psyche of the organization that even when leaders attempt to create positive change, everyone responds with cynicism and resistance.

To unfear an organization, we need to tell generative stories. There are infinite ways to do this, but these are the three that we have seen to be most effective: cathedral stories, what's in it for me, and creating positive lore out of the company's past.

Cathedral Stories

Consider this parable: An old man goes on a walk through his town on a hot summer day. He walks past a construction site and sees three men working. To each one he says, "It's so hot! What are you doing out here working?"

One man, working slowly and feeling miserable, answers, "I'm laying bricks. This is the only job I can find, but I need to earn a living to feed my family." Another man, working faster and with more energy, answers, "I'm building a wall. It's really nice, no?" The last man, working with great energy, joy, and speed, exclaims, "I'm building a cathedral!"

Each man is doing the same thing—yet the person who sees himself as building a cathedral, even though he will not see it completed in his lifetime, has so much more energy than the first two bricklayers.

To unfear an organization, you must tell cathedral stories—stories that create a powerful image of a collective goal that each individual strives for, a goal that goes beyond merely achieving profit and survival to realizing something large and significant, that every individual can connect to. This gives meaning to the work that individuals and teams do, and there is no greater source of energy in the world than meaning.

Think back to the story about John in Chapter 1. When he found out that he needed to let go of 250 employees, his first response was to make a thermometer graphic, with zero at the bottom and 250 at the top, and use it to track the people he had laid off. In that moment, all he was doing was painting a functional picture of laying bricks. In our work together, through a series of conversations and dialogues, John and his employees developed a cathedral story. They saw all their efforts and all the layoffs as an attempt to make something beautiful. They flipped a *Hunger Games* story into something more akin to *Apollo 13*. From there, they were able to achieve their goals and turn the site around to the point where they could rehire some of their workers.

This highlights a pivotal element of a cathedral story that helps to unfear both employees and the organization: it must be developed through two-way dialogue. If the CEO sits down and writes, by themselves, a gorgeous cathedral story and sends it out, the employees might not buy it. Generate these stories together to make them more powerful as instruments of transformational learning.

Whereas a cathedral story is essential to unfear an organization, it is not sufficient. Often organizations build their cathedral stories around customers and performance, but they forget the effort and sacrifices of the thousand heroes who built that cathedral. Great generative stories recognize and celebrate the heroes who participated in the journey. They speak of their sacrifice as well as their growth and learning.

What's in It for Me?

Unfear organizations take the time to tell stories about what each new program or initiative has to offer its heroes. It might be something as simple as more money and higher pay. It might be professional development, the promise of a promotion, or a new learning opportunity. The point is that when individuals feel like their needs are being honored, they are willing to step out of their comfort zone and put in the extra effort that a transformation needs from each of its thousand heroes.

Celebration and Lore

The lore of every organization is how that organization understands its past. It's the myths, history, and stories that are repeated; what events people choose to remember; and, more important, how they remember them. In a fear-based organization, the lore is usually negative. For example, one of our clients experienced a bitter battle between the union and management that led to a plant shutdown about five years before we started working with them. In our initial interviews, almost everyone we talked to told us about that fight. Employees talked about management's lack of respect, and management talked about the duplicity of the union. The remarkable thing is that 60 percent of the people we interviewed didn't even work for the plant during the shutdown. Yet that fight had become part of the company lore, so it still impacted the culture and how people showed up.

To unfear an organization, you need to consciously create a more positive lore. When you actively engage with lore, you can change the perception people have of the company and the way they show up and design a new future. When you ignore the lore, you let the past determine the future. The most important part of building an unfear lore is to celebrate individual and collective successes. By doing this, you create a more optimistic culture in which people believe that change and achievement are possible.

Another way to create unfear lore is to actively engage in the telling of failures. If you ignore or gloss over failures, you will create immediate mistrust. If you engage with failures from a place of scare mongering or punitive action, it creates a lore that inspires fear. In contrast, if you focus on the lessons that you learned from the failure, not only does it reduce fear in the organization, but it also helps everyone else reframe their relationship with fear and failure so that they learn to view both as learning experiences.

Unfear Practice 2: Create Powerful Learning Routines and Habits

Organizations coordinate the actions of tens and hundreds, if not thousands, of people in pursuit of their goals and missions. This requires a mix of disciplined action and freedom for creative thinking. All organizations have routines and habits they use to manage how work gets done. Fear-based organizations, however, may fall into some traps. One tendency in fear-based organizations is to exercise too much control and discipline in the work environment. This may generate movement toward a goal, but it doesn't create the space for people to fully participate and speak up. On the opposite end of the spectrum, in some organizations, managers avoid any attempt at control and leave people to sort out their own way of working. This results in a lack of coordination and movement toward collective goals.

Unfear organizations design routines and habits that create intentional learning moments. They use elements of disciplined action in ways that encourage people to speak up and fully participate rather than shutting them down. They use elements of freedom in ways that help employees channel their ideas and abilities toward collective outcomes. To spark your own creative thinking about routines and habits to apply in your organization, we offer two distinct learning routines to experiment with: short-cycle loops and long-cycle loops.

Short-Cycle Learning Loops

Short-cycle learning loops help people see and meet daily challenges and execute plans that last anywhere from a single shift to a couple of weeks. These loops are characterized by a clear set of expectations over a specific time frame (e.g., deliver these features in x weeks) and regular touch-points and visual tools (e.g., daily huddles, *Kanban* boards) to quickly assess progress, highlight any challenges, and plan course corrections. These elements of the routine make it easier for everyone to act in an unfear way. Because expectations are clear and shared, employees feel more comfortable speaking up and offering their own ideas regardless of hierarchy, expertise, or personality. These routines also help people learn and receive coaching from their leaders because they create a space for individuals or teams to say, "Hey, something's not right here," "I need help," or "You missed something."

These loops usually play out like this: a team sets a specific goal over a certain time period. Then every day (or every week, month, etc.), the entire team meets around a physical or virtual whiteboard that depicts the status of key metrics and priority tasks. Everyone shares an update on how their work is going. Here the entire team can quickly understand the status of the project, celebrate accomplishments, flag issues, and ask for help, if necessary. Rather than waiting an indefinite amount of time to understand whether something is off, these kinds of interactions allow people across an organization to learn and adjust more quickly and with greater confidence.

You can also create learning habits that run on even shorter cycles. For example, an increasing number of hospitals write checklists with the key actions that need to happen for a successful and safe surgical procedure. This creates a shared understanding of the target condition—that is, that everything on the checklist will be accomplished—and a time frame to realize this goal. Then it creates the conditions under which each team member can speak up and course correct the process if something seems wrong. If a nurse notices that the "Clean incision site," hasn't been checked off, he or she can bring this to the attention of the surgeon, with much less fear because that nurse *knows* that a step has been skipped and following the checklist is a norm shared by the team. In other words, the checklist makes everyone a potential expert who can contribute with their full selves in the moment, not just certain individuals with special roles or educational credentials.

> *Unfear organizations design routines and habits that create intentional learning moments.*

Long-Cycle Learning Loops

Organizations use long-cycle learning loops to provide space for deep thinking and creative play. As we mentioned in Chapter 5, our most creative thoughts usually come when we are in an alpha-theta brain state, which arises when we aren't in the busy rush of our daily work but doing something relaxing, such as showering or walking in nature. If you want an unfear workplace, where people engage in deep, creative thinking, you need to create a space that enables people to get into a less hectic state of mind. For example, Google encourages many of its employees (especially its engineers) to spend a full day of each week working on some creative, interesting project that sparks their curiosity.

Some organizations accomplish a similar result by holding multiday continuous-improvement workshops at regular intervals. Others have regularly scheduled time each week when employees come together to solve bigger problems. We saw an excellent example of this while touring Autoliv, a manufacturing plant in Utah that won the most prestigious award for operational excellence, the Shingo Prize. Each week, frontline employees shut down their area of production for a visit from engineers and other support staff. These frontline employees then describe their ideas for improving the safety and ergonomics of the production equipment, as well as the quality and productivity of their production cell. That technical team goes off to develop solutions and then presents them to the frontline workers the next week. The people closest to the value-adding work generate ideas and receive extra support in implementing them. If every organization put in place a practice such as this, it would dramatically boost continuous improvement.

Another example of these longer cycles of improvement is after-action reviews or postmortems. In his book, *Creativity, Inc.: Overcoming the Unseen Forces That Stand in the Way of True Inspiration*,[4] Ed Catmull, the CEO of Pixar, describes how his teams get together at the completion of each movie to share lessons learned. People come prepared for these meetings to talk candidly about what worked and what didn't—

not to blame others or get stuck in self-congratulatory praise, but to honestly reflect and share information so that the next movie is that much better. This process also helps to reinforce a culture in which every worker shares ideas openly and is always looking for opportunities to learn and improve.

There are countless ways to create structured space for creativity in the work environment. We offer only a few here. The specific structure of these routines is less important, however, than sustaining the learning intention behind them. You can have the best creative process in the world, but if people show up to conversations incurious, defensive about their ideas, and unwilling to say, "Wow, I don't know . . . , but let's find out," they are not likely to produce any real collective learning. Experiment with the routines and habits, but do them mindfully and with purpose.

Unfear Practice 3: Inspiring Through Action

Actions speak louder than words. This is just common sense. Yet, in so many fear-based organizations, this common sense is hardly common. In those organizations, leaders say one thing and then behave in an entirely different way. This lack of alignment increases fear and resentment in an organization because employees begin to doubt the honesty of their leaders and feel that certain rules only apply to them. There are two major nonverbal avenues that all leaders need to use to create an unfear context: role modeling and symbolic actions.

Role Modeling

Role modeling unfear behavior is a key part of any unfear transformation. When leaders decide to implement the practice and mindsets discussed herein, they have to begin with themselves first. If they don't, it will only inspire suspicion and skepticism. Employees find it unfair that they're being asked to do something that leaders aren't doing. In contrast, effective role modeling boosts employees' courage as they stumble and make mistakes while attempting new ways of doing and being. In all of this, however, it's important to remember that some actions speak louder than other actions. Effective role modeling doesn't just occur when everything is going well. It is most vital to role model positive, unfear behavior during challenging times. Because of negativity bias, people are more likely to remember what happens during a crisis than during normal operations.

For example, one of our clients, a startup, called us in because the new CEO, who had replaced a well-loved predecessor, was having a lot of trouble connecting with the team. The employees were practically in a full-blown revolt, and the company was struggling to get off the ground and launch a major product. Fear ran rampant throughout the organization. One of the first things that we invited the CEO to do was to call a meeting. Then we had him role model openness and vulnerability and share the story of his life, including the challenging events that had shaped him and led him to his current role. This proved to be a watershed moment for him and the team. Not only did it humanize him, but it also created safety for everyone to tell their own stories. Rather than powering through the revolt, the CEO slowed down and role modeled a willingness to invest in relationships. This was far from the only thing we did with that company, but it helped lay the essential groundwork to build more trust in the organization.

Symbolic Actions

Symbolic actions are actions that leaders take, small or large, that promote the narrative they want to advance. These actions can be used to tell just about any story. For example, Ray Krock, the former CEO of McDonald's, used a symbolic action to communicate the importance of cleanliness at McDonald's franchises. According to the story, he just showed up at a random McDonald's, with no fuss or warning, and started cleaning the place himself. According to employees at the time, this one act did more to enhance cleanliness at McDonald's than any other formal process could because it showed the extent to which the CEO himself was committed to that goal.

Symbolic actions can be used to emphasize any of the mindsets mentioned in the transformation learning section. For example, these actions also can demonstrate a commitment to living a company's purpose. This is exactly what the CEO of a large Australian bank did back in the 1990s. This CEO had decided to run the company in a very honest, consumer-friendly way. One quarter, the credit-card department suddenly started reporting much higher levels of revenue than it had before. The CEO called the head of the department in and asked how he had increased revenue so much. The head of credit cards didn't want to share this initially, arguing that it didn't matter and that all that mattered was the result. Eventually, the CEO got him to talk, and he revealed that he did it by increasing one of the hidden fees related to the card. The CEO instructed him to instantly refund this to all the bank's customers, write an apology, and send it to the customers. Then the bank sent out a press release about the apology to all the major newspapers.

Then the CEO fired the department head.

Actions such as this prove the depth of a company's commitment to its purpose. Even though the CEO responded with a harsh, forceful punishment, these actions don't increase fear in the workplace because the punishment is aligned with the organization's stated values. This shows employees that the company is living its values, and it helps guide their behavior. It connects them to the purpose and creates a degree of consistency that reduces fear because they don't have to worry that their superiors will act in unpredictable ways. Using this tool wisely can set the context for an unfear organization.

Unfear Practice 4: Aligning Performance Management with the Unfear Culture

Aligning performance management practices (essentially the incentive and discipline structure) with an unfear ethos is one of the biggest challenges of an unfear transformation effort. These practices usually provide tangible evidence of the extent of an organization's commitment to unfear principles. For example, if the organization says that it wants to encourage people to ask for help when they need it (vulnerability) but then rewards only independent self-starters, this may create fear and mistrust. There are some schools of thought that advocate getting rid of performance management entirely. We do not agree, but we do think that it is an infinitely complicated issue that requires much intentional thought. Organizations that want to engage in an unfear transformation need to reflect on three aspects of their performance management process: design, performance reviews, and terminations and resignations.

Design

Most organizations design their performance management systems around a few widely held core beliefs about what drives individuals and teams to perform at their best. These beliefs are so deeply entrenched that most organizations accept them as best practices, without any questions.

We invite you to reexamine your performance management architecture in the context of your desired unfear mindsets. Here are a few questions to get you started: What signals does your performance management system convey to the organization? If your performance management system is heavily oriented toward incentivizing individual performance, how does it build horizontal relationships? What are the implications of a forced ranking system on the level of fear and competitiveness within the organization? If the manager is the primary arbitrator of performance, how does one create the space for difficult conversations?

You will likely see areas where the performance management structure interferes with an unfear transformation. Once you've noticed this, you can begin to build a structure that better aligns with the culture you want to create. We recommend doing this from first principles. Identify what unfear values you want to emphasize, and then build the performance management system from there.

Even after you've redesigned the system, you will notice several contradictions. Your incentive and evaluation structure will show you the tension between different values. For example, what is more important—putting the client first or work-life balance? When these contradidions arise, do not gloss over them. Instead, force a conversation about the tradeoffs you are making. This will help sort out which values in the organization hold more weight than others and what you actually care about the most. Then, when you share the new performance management infrastructure with the organization, draw attention to these contradictions, explain the tradeoffs, and indicate why you made the decisions you did. Everyone might not agree with them, but if they understand the thought process, it will reduce fear overall.

> *The intent of the performance management system in an unfear system is not to pick winners and losers but to create a community of high-performing learners yearning to improve every day.*

Each unfear performance management system will be unique. That said, there are three guiding principles in a good design. First, remember that the intent of the performance management system in an unfear system is not to pick winners and losers but to create a community of high-performing learners yearning to improve every day. Second, make sure that you reward the *mindsets* behind an action just as much as you reward the results. For example, if somebody has a continuous-improvement mindset and makes a change that doesn't work, reward the initiative while using the experience as a coaching opportunity to help develop that employee's skills. Finally, do not consider the design of performance management a one-and-done exercise. These processes are foundational to the success of an organization. After every cycle, evaluate your evaluation processes. Reflect on the strengths and areas where improvement is needed. Then evolve the system to keep it relevant, vibrant, and aligned with the cultural values you wish to create.

Performance Reviews

The way performance reviews are delivered either reinforces the unfear ethos or destroys it. Most organizations train people on how to structure performance reviews, how to fill out forms, and how to report the results to human resources. The key to performance reviews in an unfear organization is to focus on preparing the mindset and intention of both the reviewer and reviewee. In an unfear organization, the reviewer shows up as a coach, not as a judge of performance. Reviewer and reviewee work to create awareness of the reviewee's current behavior and performance and help the reviewee choose to improve and determine how to do so. These sessions build confidence in the reviewee. In an unfear organization, the reviewee approaches the process with openness, prepared to receive feedback. The reviewee embraces the review as an opportunity to learn and grow. Additionally, in an unfear organization, instead of the reviewer mandating changes in behavior, both parties agree to a development plan that they commit to execute together.

Terminations

Most organizations don't run like families. Leaders have to make tough choices about who to hire and who to fire. Not everyone will be a good fit. Terminations often generate a tremendous amount of fear and mistrust and create significant headwinds for an organization attempting to unfear. Aggressive/Defensive organizations tend to make terminations a punishment for poor performance and a demonstration of the strength and decisiveness of leadership. Passive/Defensive organizations tend to avoid difficult personnel decisions until either the employees leave on their own or the situation becomes so unbearable that the organization finally makes a decision.

The unfear way to release people is to tie the action to the cathedral story of the organization while also respecting the needs of the individual. There is a saying: "You cannot clap with one hand." In all but the most extreme cases, when an organization lets someone go, the typical reasons given are one-sided and focused on the deficiencies of the employee. But there is a fuller story to tell here. Rather than a mark of shame for both the organization and the individual, a release from the organization is an occasion to restate the organization's values, expectations, and goals and to show respect to a person, even if he or she doesn't have a role in the organization.

Don't sugarcoat a tough message. Deliver it respectfully. Tell the individual and the rest of the organization the truth, whatever it is. It may be challenging, but delivering that difficult message in a caring way will build trust over time because people will feel like they're being leveled with. Of course, there is a caveat to this: it only works when you already have a well-established practice of engaging in difficult conversations in an effective way. If that practice exists, then you can handle the termination with dignity and respect. This is a situation in which one of your heroes is leaving because their journey is taking them elsewhere. The rest of the heroes will carry on, with resilience, in the face of whatever might come. Of course, they have to consider themselves heroes first, which requires a transformation on each level of an organization. Such a transformation can be tricky and requires a deft touch.

- Is your organization motivating others through fear or excitement?

- Are people in your company treated as adults or as children?

- What are the stories being actively told, enacted, and reinforced across the business? How do these stories perpetuate a culture of fear or unfear?

- How effectively do people learn or drive continuous improvement every day at work? What conditions in the organization help or hinder this?

- As a leader, are you role modeling invincibility or vulnerability? Is your role modeling eliciting fear or unfear in others?

- What symbolic actions can you take to build trust and inspire your organization to unfear?

8

Orchestrating the Transformation to Unfear

When a caterpillar transforms into a butterfly, it undergoes a complicated process. After fattening itself up for several weeks, the caterpillar stops eating, hangs upside down from a twig or a leaf, and spins itself a silky cocoon and molts into a shiny chrysalis. Inside, the caterpillar digests itself by releasing enzymes that dissolve all its tissue. All that remains is a sort of "caterpillar soup." Yet certain highly organized groups of cells survive this process and float in the soup. These groups of cells—called *imaginal discs*—are what will eventually become the wings, the eyes, the legs, and all the other parts of the butterfly. There is a disc for each of these parts. Caterpillars carry these discs within them from birth, but they remain dormant until juvenile hormone production declines. Once hormone levels fall below a certain threshold, the imaginal discs use the protein-rich caterpillar soup to fuel rapid cell division as they form the new butterfly.

This mirrors an organizational unfear metamorphosis. Much like a butterfly is different from a caterpillar, an unfear organization is fundamentally different from typical organizations not just in form but also in the perspective it holds. The infinite potential of ourselves, our teams, and our organizations is like the imaginal discs. They've always existed within us. Yet we also have juvenile hormones—fear and our stories around it—that keep them dormant. When we unfear ourselves, we allow the natural transformation to happen.

Like a metamorphosis, the journey to unfear is precarious and messy. We have identified five guiding principles, which we call the *five Cs*, that help us execute the transformation successfully: chaordic, co-creation, courage, critical mass, and commitment.

Chaordic

Dee Hock, founder and former CEO of Visa, coined the term *chaordic* to describe a system that blends chaos with order to create powerful outcomes. We've made a slight variation to this definition. We use chaordic to describe a system that allows for chaos to occur *within* order. In other words, this is a system that provides clear boundaries while leaving sufficient space for employees to be creative, experiment, and develop a sense of ownership of their work. The most important boundaries are a clear initial goal for the transformation and well-defined first steps. Leaders of a chaordic transformation, however, recognize that these initial targets and approaches can always change. They attempt to get everyone moving in the same direction while giving them the power to find new ways to get there.

> *A chaordic system allows for chaos to occur within order and provides clear boundaries while leaving sufficient space for employees to be creative, experiment, and develop a sense of ownership of their work.*

This is in contrast to the two prevailing schools of thought on transformations, one that overemphasizes order and the other that focuses on chaos. The school of order relies on a central project management office that makes sure that the transformation goes exactly according to plan. The project management office maintains strict control over employees and gives little freedom to deviate from the objective and steps laid out by the transformation experts. This approach to transformation relies on coercion and fear to drive compliance, which, obviously, is antithetical to an unfear transformation.

The school of chaos tries to light a thousand sparks and see which one catches fire. This approach mistakes hope for a strategy and leaves far too much to chance. It creates greater uncertainty, which also leads to more fear. A common example of this is when a company sends all its employees to different workshops or training sessions. The company might ask its employees to train in design thinking, lean, or agile, but it hasn't paired these trainings with any new systems, processes, or practices in the company. Imagine a caterpillar becoming caterpillar soup without the chrysalis. It would likely die before it became a butterfly.

Co-Creation

Leaders can never mandate from above that their employees and organization go on an unfear journey. Any attempt to do so would just create more fear. Instead, a true unfear journey relies on co-creation, where formal and informal leaders work together to transform the organization. Through dialogue, they develop the strategy, the new stories about fear and purpose, and so on. A wide range of people in the organization contributes, and everyone feels ownership over the program. When this happens, it naturally reduces fear. The transformation initiative is no longer something that happens *to* employees; instead, it's something they influence and shape. Co-creation begins when people choose to reexamine their relationship with fear as the first step on their journey to unfear themselves. Personal choice is essential for any durable shift in mindset.

> *Personal choice is essential for any durable shift in mindset.*

Leaders often summon us to their offices early in an unfear transformation to demand that the process go more quickly. They don't understand why it takes longer for some employees to understand the value in the change efforts, and they want us to get more people on board faster.

We remind these CEOs that sometimes you need to slow down to go fast. We encourage them to invest time in the beginning so that employees can come to grips with their own resistance, self-assess their mindsets, and make their own decisions. To facilitate this, we suggest that they frame the transformation effort as a request rather than a demand. Demands rely on fear to drive compliance, whereas requests open space for dialogue, creativity, and reflection. When people go through these dialogues and reflections and choose to buy in, they display a much higher level of engagement. They feel motivated to create an organization that they are proud of. When leaders accept this co-creative energy, they accelerate progress toward an unfear organization.

Courage

Unfear transformations, like life, are not linear. In the middle of a transformation, it can feel like there's no movement, as if the company isn't going forward, sideways, or even backward, as though there is no clear direction. This is the belly of the beast—the period when the organizational mindsets have liquified into soup, but the butterfly hasn't started to take shape. Every unfear journey goes through it—not once, not twice, but several times. In fact, this process never stops. As we mentioned in Chapter 7, an unfear organization is constantly on a journey, constantly in the middle of a transformation, and constantly transitioning between soup and form.

> *An unfear organization is constantly on a journey,*
> *constantly in the middle of a transformation,*
> *and constantly transitioning between soup and form.*

In this period, people often want to disengage. The uncertainty and fear reach their peak. But it is also in these moments that we can learn the most, and everyone needs the courage to lean into this discomfort. The only way to unfear is to embrace the fear, to go through it, and to discover what fear can teach us. It is in these moments that we need to have difficult conversations—with ourselves, with team members, and within the organization—that force us to look at our limiting beliefs, that invite us to reflect rather than react, and that allow us to imagine bold, audacious solutions. Leaders need to demonstrate the courage to say "I don't know" to open the door to learning something new. Leaders and organizations need to commit themselves to the process without the certainty of a definite outcome while holding the intention to achieve it and flexibly working toward it. This requires courage.

Critical Mass

As we've discussed, we cannot transform an organization by focusing only on processes, policies, systems, structures, and infrastructure. We must change the DNA: the mindsets of employees. When a critical mass of people transform their thoughts and behaviors in an organization, then the entire system will follow, seemingly overnight and on its own. This is what we mean when we say that you have to go slow to go fast. By taking the time to ensure that individuals truly embrace their new ideas, you can build momentum that will lead to rapid change.

> *When a critical mass of people transform their thoughts and behaviors in an organization, then the entire system will follow, seemingly overnight and on its own.*

Social scientists call the point at which a system changes from one state to another the *tipping point*. A perfect illustration of this is the game of Jenga. At the beginning, players remove blocks from the tower without any noticeable change to the condition of the tower. It continues to stand, until that one block is removed, and the whole tower comes tumbling down. An unfear journey follows the same process. At the start, the fear archetypes dominate everyone's behavior. Once a critical mass of people unfear themselves, the patterns of fear-based behavior come crashing down. The amazing thing about these tipping points is that they require far fewer people to buy-in than one would expect. Theoretical models of tipping points and the viral spread of ideas show that in some cases it takes just 10 percent of the people in a system to push everyone else over the threshold. In other cases, that number can be as much as 50 percent, but the bottom line is that these transformations can occur without a majority of the population.

In our experience, we've found that getting buy-in from about 30 percent of those with the most influence in a system will trigger the tipping point. Usually, this list of people differs greatly from that of the highest performers. The four most important groups to target are senior leaders, troublemakers, informal leaders, and middle managers:

- **Senior leaders.** These are the top couple of layers of an organization. Although they might only include 10 to 20 people out of hundreds or thousands of employees, they carry the most influencing power. Most people look to senior leaders to understand what it takes to be successful. How these leaders perform in times of crisis sets the tone for the entire company and will go a long way toward shaping the outcome of an unfear transformation. Senior leaders carry 10 to 15 percent of the influencing power.

- **Troublemakers.** These are the biggest gossips and almost always show up in the victim mindset. They purport to know what's really going on, usually tell stories that run counter to what senior leaders say, and develop deep relationships with other gossips/victims in the organization. Indeed, *troublemaker* only refers to how the leadership views these employees. One person's troublemaker is another person's soothsayer. Often senior leaders try to marginalize these people in any change effort. While this seems logical, it is a fallacy that stems from the knower mindset. The leaders assume that the troublemakers can never be won over, so they don't include them in their efforts. This fallacy alone can derail a transformation effort. What the leaders don't understand is that the troublemakers only raise all the objections they do is because they actually care. If they didn't, they'd just follow along. Marginalizing these energized, often charismatic workers creates a lot of fear and resistance among those close to them. The more effective approach is to intentionally include these troublemakers in any change effort. When they become active and vocal supporters, it adds tremendous momentum to the transformation.

For example, one of our clients had this old employee who was one year out from retirement and had become a very negative force in the company. Whenever somebody brought him a new idea, he'd shoot it down, saying that he'd seen everything in his career. Our clients didn't want him anywhere near the transformation effort, but we insisted that he should be one of our main change agents. At first, he resisted the program, but eventually he realized the limits that his mindsets created for him. He became a champion of the transformation effort, and the rest of the company was stunned. It became a watershed moment: everyone thought that if this man believed in the program, then maybe there was something there, and several more troublemakers bought in. People like this carry about 10 percent of influencing power.

- **Informal leaders.** These are the trusted, energetic, hard-charging employees who say the right things and can rally their peers to a cause. In finding these people, focus less on performance and more on their influence. The high performer who siloes himself or herself and has weak relationships with the rest of the organization will be far less helpful than the charismatic achiever. Informal leaders carry about 5 percent of influencing power.
- **Middle managers.** These leaders are often the concrete in an organization. They serve as vital supports and are hardened by the pressures coming from above and below. They may not create great shifts in the organization, but if they resist, the transformation will almost always fail. Because of their large numbers, they carry another about 5 to 10 percent of the influencing power in an organization.

Case Study: Waking Up Sleeping Beauty

In February 2016, in a ballroom of the Orlando Hilton, Anne Miller, Greg Pflum, and Mark Pellow let out a small shout of satisfaction. BASF Wyandotte, the chemical manufacturing site where they all served as executives, had just won the award for the Most Innovative Approach to Culture Change at the PEX Global Conference—a community of more than 30,000 practitioners of operational excellence and performance transformation. In the back of that room, I (Gaurav) did a happy dance of my own. Co-Creation Partners had just pulled off our most ambitious unfear transformation in our short six-year history.

This transformation had started in 2011, when our lead client at BASF asked us to wake up what she called their "Sleeping Beauty,"[1] the Wyandotte site. The site did seem to be asleep—it was mired in complacency and showed all the classic characteristics of a Passive/Defensive culture. Greg Pflum, the site leader, had asked us to do mindset and behavior work. He recognized that yet another operational improvement effort would not help lead to the results he desired. Instead, he wanted to get to the root of the issue. We began by working to unfear the individuals. After that, we equipped them with the framework to rapidly unfear their teams and organizations. And they did. Their success proved to us how powerful reframing our relationship with fear could be and became the basis for many of the ideas in this book.

Situation

In 2011, the aftermath of the 2008 recession coupled with new domestic and foreign competition posed a serious threat to BASF Wyandotte's financial safety. Five of the seven plants were in the red, yet the site had been around for decades, so employees did not see a need to do things differently. At the same time, silos prevented knowledge sharing across the site. Everyone was stuck in fear and a survival orientation. In response, a corporate-driven operational excellence site assessment had identified 43 projects to improve operational performance and generate $6.6 million in savings—a pretty standard response given the situation.

Approach

Wyandotte decided to take a different approach. Pflum could tell that there were some serious cultural issues holding the site back. At the outset, we created the space for a chaordic process by identifying a set of four themes that became the guideposts for the transformation (Table 8.1).

With us, the site embarked on a sustained campaign to unfear (though at the time we didn't call it that) individuals, foster understanding of and conviction in the transformation, role model desired behaviors, reinforce day-to-day continuous improvement by implementing learning routines, develop diverse action learning skills, and communicate in a new way. We launched the program with transformation learning workshops for both formal and informal leaders.

TABLE 8.1 The Wyandotte Journey

Results | Culture Shift

FROM	TO
Silos Nobody talked to people outside their immediate networks. People didn't know who their counterparts were in other plants on the site.	**People CARE** People want to help one another and feel comfortable reaching out to coworkers because they trust those coworkers will want to help.
Same Old, Same Old People didn't try new things. "If you had an idea, maybe you thought your boss wouldn't support you, or maybe you didn't know who to ask about how to implement this, or you'd be punished for failure, or you didn't trust that you'd ever get any money, so you just didn't do it." *— Wyandotte employee*	**People TALK** Wyandotte has a very collaborative environment where people consistently reach out for help. "Instead of worrying about your little bubble, it's turned into something for the greater good." *— Wyandotte employee*
"Straight Eight" People did the bare minimum required. "You were here to work straight eight and then get out." The attitude was, "Just tell me what you want me to do, and I'm gonna do it and go home." *— Wyandotte employee; OpEx Site Lead*	**People TRY NEW THINGS** People feel their work is part of them. Leaders and managers are more willing to support not only ideas, but failures. The attitude is, "Try something! If that doesn't work, we'll try something else…We're here to make things better." *— Wyandotte employee*
Blame "People focused on who else's fault it was, why it's not my fault, it was the engineer's fault, or the manager's fault, etc." *— OpEx Site Lead*	**People TAKE OWNERSHIP** The ownership factor "is way up"; employees suggest improvements and lead projects. *— OpEx Site Lead*

Leadership Guidance

Part of why this transformation was so successful is that we reached a point of critical mass early on: we worked with around 70 people in the first 100 days. These included senior leaders, troublemakers, informal leaders, and middle managers.

It all started with Anne Miller, an executive and organizational development expert, and Mark Pellow, an executive and operational excellence expert. Anne and Mark agreed to guide the effort and threw themselves into it with enthusiasm. They oversaw and coordinated various initiatives, coached other senior leaders and work groups, and supported the change architecture. Together they created and maintained the right boundaries that allowed the chaordic transformation to flourish.

Other critical business leaders—senior vice presidents, vice presidents, directors, and plant managers—committed to the transformation. As part of that, they committed to reframing their relationships with fear in a very visible way. In meetings, they role modeled new unfear techniques, applied the mastery and learner mindsets, and used unfear language. They developed rituals to celebrate the change agents and change catalysts who unfeared themselves and committed to continuous improvement.

Co-Creating with Informal Leaders

Mark, Anne, and the other formal leaders committed to co-creating the transformation with the informal leaders. First, they enabled an environment that would allow people to unfear themselves, to recognize their unlimited potential, and to step into the mastery and learner mindsets. They did this through workshops, conversations, and, ultimately, patience. They gave their employees time to self-discover their nonproductive relationship with fear and to choose to shift out of it.

It took real courage for Greg, Anne, and Mark to stay the course even as they were barraged by the cynicism of troublemakers. These troublemakers second-guessed every action and looked for ulterior motives in every decision. For us, this behavior was normal. We understood that the journey to unfear involves going through a visceral experience of fear. For our clients, this was a deeply uncomfortable experience.

After that, several employees volunteered their time to work in focus teams with Anne and Mark to co-create an unfear culture for the site. The focus teams not only identified improvement opportunities but also worked to boost energy, provide continued education, and spread the change.

The path for focus teams was neither easy nor straightforward. They had to figure out how to engage the site in their work, how to deal with resistance, and how to communicate the unfear language. They experimented with a lot of ideas, they stumbled, and sometimes no one showed up. Yet, with courage and support, they built a resilient program.

Ten years later, the focus teams continue to operate. Participants rotate in and out based on interest. Each focus team has a transition plan to ensure continuity and sustain energy even as participants change. In a gathering of about 60 people each year, focus team leaders and the site's senior executives participate in a joint review of the program's architecture, vision, and goals. In these meetings, they continue the co-creation process and tweak the program as necessary.

Impact

The tangible impact of the program is summarized below.

1. **Profitability.** By 2016, all seven plants were back in the black with near-specialty margins. The site invested in every facility, and investments totaled over $100 million in four years.
2. **Savings.** In 2016, when BASF Wyandotte won the PEX Award, the site had saved over $50 million. Prior to our program, an outside estimate projected savings of $6 million. The unfear program ultimately delivered results seven times greater than expected. The program continues to go from strength to strength to this day.
3. **Operational excellence improvement database.** Employees expanded on the initial 43 recommendations and built a database

to track improvement projects. In 2016, they had documented 528 improvements, of which 364 had been closed and 164 were open and underway.

4. **Growth.** The site added 270 new jobs over four years (>25 percent increase) and expanded to use all available space on the site.

5. **Unfear culture.** The culture shifted from one of silos, complacency, and resistance to one with a continuous-improvement mindset, high employee ownership of initiatives, and strong cross-business collaboration.

The best way to bring this to life is to share a few employee testimonials:

- "Instead of worrying about your little bubble, it's turned into something for the greater good."
- "Try something! If that does not work, we'll try something else. . . . We're here to make things better."
- "The ownership factor is way up. We suggest improvements, and we lead the way."

A Personal Note

Our involvement at the Wyandotte site is now limited to the occasional workshop to support a specific initiative. Every time we visit, the employees meet us with sparkling eyes, hugs, and high fives. People reminisce affectionately about their transformative experiences, but they also remember how painful the transformation felt and how much courage it took for them to navigate it.

For us, this is the greatest joy. Our work often takes us on the road and away from our families, which can be very difficult. Yet we know that each time we start a project, we add to our extended family and build relationships that we know will stand the test of time. We may not speak to these people for years, and yet the moment we meet again, it is as if we were never apart. The thousands of people who have been through our workshops, who have traveled with us on this journey, are our greatest teachers and friends.

- What might an unfear journey look like for your organization?
- How might an inside-out transformation be different from what you've tried in other improvement efforts?
- What steps are you ready to take to unfear your organization?
- How might your own fears guide you in taking these steps?

Epilogue

usinesses impact human lives in profound and persistent ways, and this impact will only continue to grow. More and more people work for large corporations as a share of overall employment. The bigger companies keep getting bigger. And they mediate virtually everything we interact with on any given day. However, for all that interaction, the net impact of business on our human well-being is mixed. There are certainly benefits. As consumers, we reap the benefits of new products and services. As employees, we have opportunities to demonstrate our skills, challenges that help us grow, and meaningful ways to contribute to causes larger than ourselves. As communities, both local and global, we benefit from economic activity generated by business, which allows for more people to build and share wealth.

But there are also significant drawbacks. Human well-being, at least in developed countries, seems to be leveling off or even declining. Despite a proliferation of information, we seem less informed and less capable of understanding people who hold different points of view. Despite massive options for consumer goods and entertainment, we're as unhappy and unsatisfied as ever. Despite rich employment opportunities, we feel as if we're one small step away from financial ruin. Despite the most advanced healthcare in the world, we struggle to find adequate health and wellness. And we are slowly destroying the world we live in.

Fear sits at the root of many of these negative impacts. To counter these disheartening trends, we need businesses to transform. We need to unfear the world, to find a way to achieve amazing goals while maximizing our well-being, protecting our environment, and creating a healthier, more stable future for all.

Just as an organizational transformation requires a critical mass of individuals, transforming the world requires a critical mass of influencers. And businesses are part of this. If we are to shift out of fear on a global scale, we need our organizations to shift as well, to start operating in a more mindful way.

Not only are unfear organizations nimble, resilient, and innovative in an ever-changing and uncertain business environment, but they also create a ripple effect of human well-being far beyond their boundaries. First, unfear organizations enhance the well-being of their employees. This doesn't just apply while employees are "on the clock" but extends to their whole lives. It's exceptionally uncommon for people to separate the chronic stress and fear they experience at work from the rest of their lives (and vice versa), so this means that unfear organizations improve not only the personal lives of their employees but also those of their families. When people can show up as their authentic full selves at work and contribute meaningfully despite the inevitable challenges, they do so as well with their spouses, children, parents, and friends.

Second, unfear businesses impact the well-being of customers and consumers. When businesses start thinking horizontally, for instance, they aren't just focused on profit but also on how their goods and services are benefiting others.

Lastly, unfear businesses impact society—both locally and globally. They don't see good business as an either/or proposition but as a both/and proposition. We're fast discovering that everything is interconnected. Businesses can't succeed at the expense of destroying the physical and social environments that allow them to operate and thrive in the first place. Unfear organizations make different choices that result in more responsibility and accountability; greater diversity, equity, and inclusion; better safety and standards; and less waste and pollution in the communities in which they operate.

This all still starts with *you*, the individual. When we transform ourselves, we gain the capacity to transform the world around us.

We send you off on your unfear journey with some words of wisdom from a stranger. Each year, our company goes on a retreat to various parts of the world to learn about different cultures and spiritual traditions. On one of our trips, we visited South Africa. We were on a hike in a forest when we came across a barefoot man who lived there. His name was Martin. We stopped to talk, and he asked us about our work. When we told him the subject matter of our book, he nodded and said with earnest excitement, "Yes. Fear is just love that's forgotten itself, fellas. Good luck!"

Appendix

Fear/Unfear Archetypes and the Human Synergistics Circumplex

We have extensively used two survey tools from Human Synergistics International in our organizational development work within the US and across the globe. These are:

- **Organization Culture Inventory® (OCI®):** used to assess the culture of an organization in terms of behavioral norms and expectations (Current Culture) and shared values (Ideal Culture)
- **Life Styles Inventory™ (LSI):** used to assess the personal orientations of individual members and leaders in terms of their thinking and behavioral styles

These surveys are part of Human Synergistics' multilevel diagnostic system for organizational change and development. Their integrated set of complementary surveys includes not only the OCI and LSI but also inventories for groups, managers, and leaders. At the heart of these tools is the Circumplex, which breaks down and organizes the factors underlying performance (at the individual, group, and organizational levels) in terms of 12 behaviors or styles. The styles measured by the surveys are defined by and arranged in terms of two underlying dimensions. The first distinguishes between a concern for *people* (right side) versus a concern for *tasks* (left side). The second dimension distinguishes between styles directed toward fulfilling higher-order *satisfaction needs* (top) versus those directed toward protecting and maintaining lower-order *security needs* (bottom). These styles are further grouped into three general clusters: Constructive, Passive/Defensive, and Aggressive/Defensive.

The Human Synergistics Circumplex

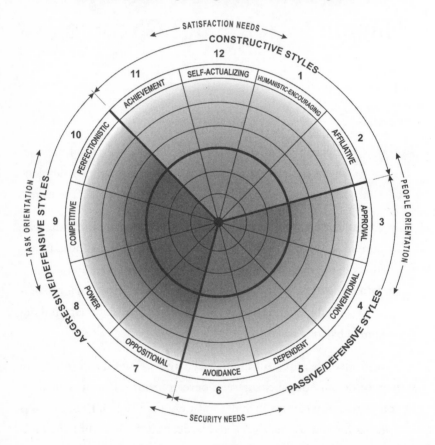

The various surveys measure the strength of the 12 styles in different ways. As noted, the Life Styles Inventory assesses the frequency with which each of the styles characterizes the thinking and behavior of individual members. At the team level, the Group Styles Inventory measures the extent to which the styles reflect the way members interact with one another and approach tasks when solving problems. The inventories for leaders and managers measure their impact on the people around them in terms of the 12 styles—as well as the factors leading to their impact. These styles are described in terms of norms and expectations as measured by the Organizational Culture Inventory.

Methodology

OCI instructions: Please think about what it takes for you and people like yourself (e.g., your coworkers, people in similar positions) to "fit in" and meet expectations in your organization. Selecting from the response options below, indicate the extent to which each of the following behaviors is expected.

Response Options

1. Not at all
2. To a slight extent
3. To a moderate extent
4. To a great extent
5. To a very great extent

To what extent are people expected or implicitly required to . . .

Descriptions of the 12 Styles Measured by the Organizational Culture Inventory® (and Sample Items)

Constructive Norms (11 o'clock to 2 o'clock—Cultural Styles Promoting Satisfaction Behaviors)

Achievement

An Achievement culture characterizes organizations that do things well and value members who set and accomplish their own goals. Members are expected to set challenging but realistic goals, establish plans to reach these goals, and pursue them with enthusiasm. *(Pursue a standard of excellence; openly show enthusiasm.)*

Self-Actualizing

A Self-Actualizing culture characterizes organizations that value creativity, quality over quantity, and both task accomplishment and individual growth. Members are encouraged to gain enjoyment from their work, develop themselves, and take on new and interesting activities. *(Think in unique and independent ways; do even simple tasks well.)*

Humanistic-Encouraging

A Humanistic-Encouraging culture characterizes organizations that are managed in a participative and person-centered way. Members are expected to be supportive, constructive, and open to influence in their dealings with one another. *(Help others to grow and develop; take time with people.)*

Affiliative

An Affiliative culture characterizes organizations that place a high priority on constructive interpersonal relationships. Members are expected to be friendly, open, and sensitive to the satisfaction of their work group. *(Deal with others in a friendly, pleasant way; share feelings and thoughts.)*

Passive/Defensive Norms (3 o'clock to 6 o'clock—Cultural Styles Promoting People/Security Behaviors)

Approval

An Approval culture describes organizations in which conflicts are avoided and interpersonal relationships are pleasant—at least superficially. Members feel that they should agree with, gain the approval of, and be liked by others. *("Go along" with others; be liked by everyone.)*

Conventional

A Conventional culture is descriptive of organizations that are conservative, traditional, and bureaucratically controlled. Members are expected to conform, follow the rules, and make a good impression. *(Always follow policies and practices; fit into the "mold.")*

Dependent

A Dependent culture is descriptive of organizations that are hierarchically controlled and do not empower their members. Centralized decision-making in such organizations leads members to do only what they are told and to clear all decisions with superiors. *(Please those in positions of authority; do what is expected.)*

Avoidance

An Avoidance culture characterizes organizations that fail to reward success but nevertheless punish mistakes. This negative reward system leads members to shift responsibilities to others and avoid any possibility of being blamed for a mistake. *(Wait for others to act first; take few chances.)*

Aggressive/Defensive Norms (7 o'clock to 10 o'clock—Cultural Styles Promoting Task/Security Behaviors)

Oppositional

An Oppositional culture describes organizations in which confrontation and negativism are rewarded. Members gain status and influence by being critical and thus are reinforced to oppose the ideas of others. *(Point out flaws; be hard to impress.)*

Power

A Power culture is descriptive of nonparticipative organizations structured on the basis of the authority inherent in members' positions. Members believe they will be rewarded for taking charge, controlling subordinates, and being responsive to the demands of superiors. *(Build up one's power base; demand loyalty.)*

Competitive

A Competitive culture is one in which winning is valued and members are rewarded for outperforming one another. Members operate in a "win-lose" framework and believe they must work against (rather than with) their peers to be noticed. *(Turn the job into a contest; never appear to lose.)*

Perfectionistic

A Perfectionistic culture characterizes organizations in which perfectionism, persistence, and hard work are valued. Members feel they must avoid any mistakes, keep track of everything, and work long hours to attain narrowly defined objectives. *(Do things perfectly; keep on top of everything.)*

Research carried out over the years has consistently shown that from the individual to the organizational level, the Constructive styles are positively and significantly related to effectiveness. In contrast, the Passive/Defensive styles are generally negatively related to desired outcomes. The

The Unfear Archetypes Mapped to the Human Synergistics Circumplex

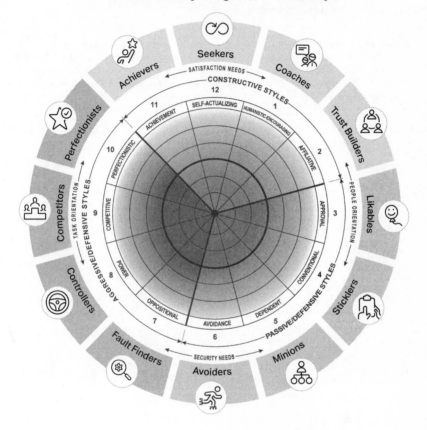

The Organization Culture Inventory Circumplex is copyrighted by, and used with the permission of, Human Synergistics.

Aggressive/Defensive styles are, at best, related to different measures of performance in mixed, inconsistent, and sometimes unexpectedly detrimental ways. Thus, development initiatives that enable organizations and their members to move from Defensive (Fear) to Constructive (Unfear) styles promote not only individual well-being and performance but also organizational effectiveness and sustainability. While the OCI and LSI tools uniquely focus on security and satisfaction norms and behaviors within organizations, they and the Fear and Unfear archetypes are parallel and powerfully complementary—and are thus the survey tools of choice for Co-Creation's work.

Notes

Introduction

1. Geoff Mead, *Telling the Story: The Heart and Soul of Successful Leadership* (San Francisco: Jossey-Bass, 2014).

Chapter 1

1. Dictionary.com.

2. University College London. "Uncertainty Can Cause More Stress Than Inevitable Pain: Knowing That There Is a Small Chance of Getting a Painful Electric Shock Can Lead to Significantly More Stress Than Knowing That You Will Definitely Be Shocked." *ScienceDaily*, March 29, 2016, www.sciencedaily.com/releases/2016/03/160329101037.htm.

3. Edmondson, Amy C., *The Fearless Organization: Creating Psychological Safety in the Workplace for Learning, Innovation, and Growth* (Wiley, November 14, 2018).

4. Jeffers, Susan, PhD, *Feel the Fear and Do It Anyway®: Dynamic Techniques for Turning Fear, Indecision and Anger into Power, Action, and Love* (Jeffers Press, April 1, 2007).

5. International Data Corporation, "Worldwide Spending on Digital Transformation Will Reach $2.3 Trillion in 2023, More Than Half of All ICT Spending, According to a New IDC Spending Guide," IDC Worldwide Semiannual Digital Transformation Spending Guide, October 28, 2019, www.idc.com/getdoc.jsp?containerId=prUS45612419.

6. Patrick Forth, Tom Reichert, Romain de Laubier, and Saibal Chakraborty, "Flipping the Odds of Digital Transformation Success," Boston Consulting Group, October 29, 2020, bcg-flipping-the-odds-of-digital -transformation-success-oct-2020.pdf.

7. Patrick Forth et al., "Flipping the Odds of Digital Transformation Success," p. 7.

8. Patrick Forth et al., "Flipping the Odds of Digital Transformation Success," p. 1.

9. Richard Barrett, *Liberating the Corporate Soul: Building a Visionary Organization* (Routledge, November 24, 2015).

10. Sundiatu Dixon-Fyle, Kevin Dolan, Vivian Hunt, and Sara Prince, "Diversity Wins: How Inclusion Matters," McKinsey & Company, May 19, 2020, www.mckinsey.com/featured-insights/diversity-and-inclusion/ diversity-wins-how-inclusion-matters.

11. Dave Bookbinder, *The NEW ROI: Return on Individuals: Do You Believe That People Are Your Company's Most Valuable Asset?* (Limelight Publishing, September 18, 2017), https://newroi.com/.

12. Daniel Kahneman, *Thinking, Fast and Slow* (Farrar, Straus and Giroux; 1st edition, October 25, 2011).

13. Kim Scott, *Radical Candor: Be a Kick-Ass Boss Without Losing Your Humanity* (St. Martins Press, October 1, 2019).

Chapter 2

1. Joseph LeDoux, *Anxious: Using the Brain to Understand and Treat Fear and Anxiety* (New York: Penguin Books, 2016).

2. James Clear, *Atomic Habits* (New York: Avery, 2018).

3. Sigal Barsade, "The Contagion We Can Control," *Harvard Business Review*, March 20, 2020, available at https://hbr.org/2020/03/the -contagion-we-can-control.

4. Barrett Values Center, Global Culture Assessment. Waynesville, NC, May 2020, www.valuescentre.com/covid/.

5. Carolyn Centeno Milton and Wendy Suzuki, "Fear Shrinks Your Brain and Makes You Less Creative." forbes.com, April 18, 2018, www.forbes .com/sites/carolyncenteno/2018/04/18/fear-shrinks-your-brain-and -makes-you-less-creative/?sh=29d5e5f11c6d.

6. Kevin Weitz, "The Neuroscience of Organizational Culture." Library of Professional Psychology, December 9, 2014, https://library.psychology. edu/the-neuroscience-of-organizational-culture/.

7. Agnese Mariotti, "The Effects of Chronic Stress on Health: New Insights Into the Molecular Mechanisms of Brain–Body Communication." US National Library of Medicine, National Institutes of Health, Bethesda, MD, November 1, 2015, www.ncbi.nlm.nih.gov/pmc/articles/PMC5137 920/.

8. Human Resources and Services Administration's 2016 National Survey of Children's Health (NSCH), Aces Fact Sheet, May 2019, www.cahmi.org/wp-content/uploads/2018/05/aces_fact_sheet.pdf.

9. Malcolm Gladwell, *Outliers: The Story of Success* (Boston: Little Brown, 2008), p. 197.

10. Chad J. Donohue, Mattew F. Glasser, Todd M. Preuss, James K. Rilling, and David C. Van Essen, "Quantitative Assessment of Prefrontal Cortex in Humans Relative to Nonhuman Primates." *Proceedings of the National Academy of Sciences of the United States of America*, May 29, 2018, www.pnas.org/content/115/22/E5183.

Chapter 3

1. Robert A. Cooke and Janet L. Szumal. "Using the Organizational Culture Inventory to Understand the Operating Cultures of Organizations," in Neal M. Ashkanasy, Celeste P.M. Wilderom, Mark F. Peterson (eds.), *Handbook of Organizational Culture & Climate* (Sage Publications, 2000).

2. The Fault Finders archetype corresponds to Oppositional (Style 7) on the Human Synergistics Circumplex.

3. The Controllers archetype corresponds to Power (Style 8) on the Human Synergistics Circumplex.

4. The Competitors archetype corresponds to Competitive (Style 9) on the Human Synergistics Circumplex.

5. The Perfectionists archetype corresponds to Perfectionistic (Style 10) on the Human Synergistics Circumplex.

6. Walter Isaacson, *Steve Jobs* (Simon & Schuster; October 24, 2011).

7. The Avoiders archetype corresponds to Avoidance (Style 6) on the Human Synergistics Circumplex.

8. The Minions archetype corresponds to Dependent (Style 5) on the Human Synergistics Circumplex.

9. The Sticklers archetype corresponds to Conventional (Style 4) on the Human Synergistics Circumplex.

10. The Likables archetype corresponds to Approval (Style 3) on the Human Synergistics Circumplex.

11. Jerry Harvey, "The Abilene Paradox: The Management of Agreement," Organizational Management, American Management Association 17(1): 19–20, 1988. doi:10.1016/0090-2616(88)90028-9.

Chapter 4

1. Taken from John Carey (ed), *Eyewitness to History* (New York: Avon, 1987), pp. 501–504.

2. Janet L Szumal and Robert A. Cooke, *Creating Constructive Cultures* (Chicago: Human Synergistics International, January 1, 2019). Available at www.humansynergistics.com.

3. The Seekers archetype corresponds to Self Actualizing (Style 12) on the Human Synergistics Circumplex.

4. Drake Baer, "13 Qualities Google Looks for in Job Candidates." *Business Insider*, April 27, 2015. Available at https://www.businessinsider.com/what-google-looks-for-in-employees-2015-4.

5. Chris Matyszczyk, "Google Can No Longer Innovate, Says Former Engineer," Cnet, January 24, 2018. Available at https://www.hci.org/session/googles-g2g-googlers-googlers-program-lesson-community-culture-and-trust.

6. The Coaches archetype corresponds to Humanistic/Encouraging (Style 1) on the Human Synergistics Circumplex.

7. Katie Anderson, *Learning to LEAD, Leading to LEARN: Lessons from Toyota Leader Isao Yoshino on a Lifetime of Continuous Learning* (Pittsburgh, PA: Integrand Press, 2020).

8. The Trust Builders archetype corresponds to Affiliative (Style 2) on the Human Synergistics Circumplex.

9. Richard Sheridan, *Joy, Inc.: How We Built a Workplace People Love* (New York: Portfolio/Penguin, 2013).

10. The Achievers archetype corresponds to Achievement (Style 11) on the Human Synergistics Circumplex.

11. Available at https://www.forbes.com/sites/quora/2017/11/08/i-worked-at-spacex-and-this-is-how-elon-musk-inspired-a-culture-of-top-performers/?sh=7dab88a4438f.

12. John P. Kotter, *Leading Change* (Boston: Harvard Business Review Press, 2012).

13. McKinsey & Company, "How to Beat the Transformation Odds," Survey, April 1, 2015. Available at https://www.mckinsey.com/business-functions/organization/our-insights/how-to-beat-the-transformation-odds.

Chapter 5

1. I found out later that she had been given the name by her Indian spiritual teacher.

2. G. K. Chesterton, *Orthodoxy* (1908), Chapter VII.

3. Plato. *Plato in Twelve Volumes*, Vol. 1 Apology, translated by Harold North Fowler; Introduction by W.R.M. Lamb (Cambridge, MA, Harvard University Press; London, William Heinemann Ltd. 1966).

4. Jung, C.G, *C.G. Jung Letters*, Vol. 1: 1906–1950 (Princeton University Press, January 1, 1973), p 33.

5. Gautama Buddha, *Dhammapada*, Chapter 6 (Pandita), Verse 80.

6. Emmet John Hughes, *The Ordeal of Power: A Political Memoir of the Eisenhower Years* (Athenaeum, January 1, 1963), p.124.

7. Viktor E. Frankl, *Man's Search for Meaning*, rev. ed. (Boston: Beacon Press, 2014), p. 75.

8. C. G. Jung (author), Aniela Jaffe (editor), Clara Winston (Translator), Richard Winston (translator), *Memories, Dreams, Reflections* (Vintage, April 23, 1989), pp 246–247.

9. William Petri, "COVID-19 Vaccines Were Developed in Record Time— but Are These Game-Changers Safe?," *The Coversation*, November 2020, https://theconversation.com/covid-19-vaccines-were-developed-in -record-time-but-are-these-game-changers-safe-150249#:~:text=The %20mRNA%20vaccines%20produced%20by,weakened%20 pathogen%20for%20the%20vaccine; Jocelyn Solis Moreira, "How Did We Develop a COVID-19 Vaccine So Quickly?," *Medical News Today*, December 15, 2020, https://www.medicalnewstoday.com/articles/how -did-we-develop-a-covid-19-vaccine-so-quickly#mRNA-technology.

10. Ned Hermann, "What Is the Function of the Various Brainwaves?," *Scientific American*, December 22, 1997, https://www.scientificamerican .com/article/what-is-the-function-of-t-1997-12-22/; Anna Wise, *The High-Performance Mind: Mastering Brainwaves for Insight, Healing, and Creativity* (New York: TarcherPerigee, 1997).

Chapter 6

1. Robert. A. Burton, MD, *On Being Certain: Believing You Are Right Even When You're Not* (St. Martin's Griffin, March 17, 2009).

2. E. F. Schumacher, *A Guide for the Perplexed* (Harper Perennial November 17, 2015).

3. Chalmers Brothers, Vinay Kumar, *Language and the Pursuit of Leadership Excellence: How Extraordinary Leaders Build Relationships, Shape Culture and Drive Breakthrough Results* (New York: New Possibilities Press, 2018).

4. Douglas Stone, Bruce Patton, Sheila Heen, *Difficult Conversations: How to Discuss What Matters Most* (Penguin Books, November 2, 2010).

5. Douglas Stone, et al., *Difficult Conversations*.

6. William R Miller, Stephen Rollnick, *Motivational Interviewing: Helping People Change* (The Guilford Press, September 7, 2012), p. 395.

Chapter 7

1. Joseph Campbell, *Hero with a Thousand Faces (The Collected Work of Joseph Campbell)*, 3rd ed. (New York: Joseph Campbell Foundation, 2020).

2. Peter Senge, *The Fifth Discipline* (New York: Doubleday Business, 1990), p. 140.

3. Jacob Botter and Lars Kolind, *Unboss* (Copenhagen: Jyllands-Postens Forlag, 2012).

4. Ed Catmull and Amy Wallace, *Creativity, Inc.: Overcoming the Unseen Forces That Stand in the Way of True Inspiration* (New York: Random House, 2014).

Chapter 8

1. Gaurav Bhatnagar and Heather Gilmartin Adams, "Contributions from Greg Pflum, Anne Miller, Mark Pellow (BASF Corporation): The Future of Operational Excellence," Co-Creation Partners, January 2017, https://cocreationpartners.com/white_paper_article/the-future-of-operational-excellence/.

Index

Page numbers followed by *f* indicate figures; *t* indicate tables.

About the Authors

Gaurav Bhatnagar is the founder of Co-Creation Partners and has dedicated more than two decades to helping companies thrive and achieve breakthrough performance. Since founding Co-Creation Partners in 2010, Gaurav has designed and led performance and culture transformations for private, public, and social-sector clients across multiple industries, including financial services, basic materials, manufacturing, healthcare, and technology. Prior to founding Co-Creation Partners, Gaurav was a consultant with McKinsey and Company, most recently as a leader in their organization practice in North America. Before McKinsey, Gaurav worked in marketing for Pepsi Cola International in Europe, the Middle East, and North Africa and for Procter & Gamble in India.

Mark Minukas is the managing partner of Co-Creation Partners. An engineer by training, Mark began his career as a Navy officer and member of the US Naval Construction Battalions (Seabees) and the Navy Dive Community. In 2005, Mark brought his experience and insights into the performance of engineered systems to McKinsey and Company, where he worked as a consultant and member of the Operations Practice. There he mastered the technical aspects of organizational transformation and process improvement, as well as the cultural side of transformation. Since leaving McKinsey to join Co-Creation Partners, Mark has worked across multiple industries, including financial services, manufacturing, information technology services, and governmental offices to deliver both top- and bottom-line improvements and build high-performing operations.

For more information, please visit unfearbook.com
and cocreationpartners.com.